GAMECOCK
GLORY

TRAVIS HANEY

GAMECOCK
GLORY

THE UNIVERSITY OF SOUTH CAROLINA
BASEBALL TEAM'S JOURNEY TO THE
2010 NCAA CHAMPIONSHIP

forewords by
MARK CALVI & CHAD HOLBROOK

THE
History
PRESS

Published by The History Press
Charleston, SC 29403
www.historypress.net

Front cover image courtesy of *Omaha World-Herald*.
All back cover images except for photograph of Teal family
courtesy of Juan Blas/TheBigSpur.com

First published 2011
Second printing 2011

ISBN 978.1.60949.254.0

Library of Congress Cataloging-in-Publication Data
Haney, Travis.
Gamecock glory : the University of South Carolina baseball team's journey to the
2010 NCAA championship / Travis Haney.
p. cm.
ISBN 978-1-54020-585-8
1. University of South Carolina--Baseball--History. 2. South Carolina Gamecocks
(Baseball team) 3. College World Series (Baseball) (2010) I. Title.
GV875.12.U75H36 2011
796.357'630975771--dc22
2011003456

In memoriam:
Herman Madden and Bayler Teal, called home in 2010.
Through Christ's love, you live on.

CONTENTS

CONTENTS

FOREWORD

Don't trip, don't trip, don't trip!"

That was all I kept saying to myself as I sprinted to join the dog pile that was forming on the mound at Coastal Carolina. What a feeling. I felt the weight of seventeen years, and hundreds of former players, lifted from my back. I got up and hugged everybody I could get my hands on. I then looked for the two most important people in my life, my wife, Kaylie, and daughter, Taylor. They had sneaked by security over the dugout and bolted for the field. As I hugged my wife, I felt the long, hard and fantastic years of this crazy profession just blend into one moment. We were finally going to Omaha. It was worth it! There had been times when I wasn't sure.

The 2010 team made it easy to see it was worth it. All the hours, days and nights on the road, recruiting or helping recruit these players, was all worth it. This team had talent, personality, attitude and a toughness that wore other teams down. It was especially evident when we played teams like Oklahoma, Arizona State, Clemson and UCLA. You can debate talent all you want, but our kids believed they were the best. Many may say it, but few believe it. All twenty-seven players moved in the same direction with a burning desire to win. What made this team so special is the way it responded to losing. All teams respond well to winning. True winners find a way to turn a loss into a victory. It would have been so easy to say, "Well, it was a great season" after the Florida series and the SEC Tournament. They bonded together even tighter. They played for each other and the program. There were no names on the back of their jerseys by the end of the season—only the name on the front.

As Scott Wingo touched home plate in Omaha, this time I watched the dog pile form. It was theirs. A team with pitchers who had ice water in their veins, and a group of hard-nosed position players with a flair for the dramatic, had done the unthinkable. A group of kids from all sorts of walks of life were now national champions. To them, I say thank you from the bottom of my heart. Aside from my daughter being born, you have given me the greatest moment in my life. It was an honor to be around you guys. I will always love each and every one of you.

I know that even if I had tripped, one of you would have picked me up.

Mark Calvi
South Carolina pitching coach, 2005–10

FOREWORD

When Coach Tanner gave me the bunt-for-base-hit sign, to give to Scott Wingo, it was the first time in my coaching career during a game that I felt a little uptight. We were a pitch away from having the leadoff hitter on base with no one out. Then, as a coach, your mind starts racing. You actually stop, just for a second, and think about the fact that you are in the national championship series against UCLA. You think, "This could be our chance, maybe our only chance, to win the national championship." It was shaping up to be the opportunity of a lifetime for our coaches, our players, our families, the university and the state of South Carolina. "This could be it," I remember thinking. "We may never, ever get this opportunity again."

"Ball four!"

The heart starts racing a little faster, the anxiety level picks up. We were three bases away from history. Two hundred and seventy feet. Next up was Evan Marzilli, a freshman. The tension on the field could be cut with a knife. You could feel it and you could see it on all the players' faces. Sure, there was pressure on UCLA, but there was also pressure on Evan to get the bunt down. After the first pitch got by the catcher and went to the backstop, you could tell Evan was relieved as Scott got to second, 180 feet from home plate and a national title. That wild pitch relaxed him. The odds were now in our favor. We kept the sacrifice bunt on because it was so important to get that runner to third base with fewer than two outs, with two of our best hitters coming up, Whit Merrifield and Jackie Bradley

Jr. After one unsuccessful attempt, Evan laid down a perfect sacrifice to advance Wingo to third, to me in the third base coaching box.

Ninety feet away. We were ninety feet away from burying some curse I had heard so much about. So many things were going through my mind. How was UCLA going to play this? With one out, would the Bruins walk Whit and Jackie to set up the double play? Or would they pitch to Whit and take their chances? Wingo and I may have looked like cool customers at third base before the pitcher toed the rubber, but I'm here to tell you we weren't. I had to tell Wingo so many things, but it was important to me that he heard one thing in particular: "No matter what, react back to third base on a line drive. We have to be in position to tag up if the ball's caught." I played out so many scenarios in my mind in the seconds before the count on Merrifield got to 2-0. I thought, "If it's a shallow fly ball, do I send Wingo? High chopper in the infield, do I send him? Swinging bunt in front of the plate, do we try to score?" All of those thoughts, and so many more, were going through my head. Then two things hit me, seconds before the 2-0 pitch was thrown, that calmed me down. The first thought was that there was no way they were going to let Jackie, the College World Series MVP, have a chance to win the game. They would walk him no matter what. As a coach, that told me that we had to be aggressive at third. If Whit hit a shallow fly ball, I had to send Scott because they were not going to let Jackie hit. Slow roller, swinging bunt or shallow fly ball off Merrifield's bat, and we were going to try to score. This was our chance.

The other thought that set me at peace, one completely different, was seven-year-old Bayler Teal. For some reason, in that moment, I thought of him. He had died late in the previous week, on the same night we needed twelve innings to beat Oklahoma. That little guy, fighting cancer, put things in perspective for all of us. I knew his parents, Rob and Risha, were in attendance. I knew Bayler was looking out for us. He was not going to let us lose, and that was comforting.

As the 2-0 pitch left the pitcher's right hand, everything looked good. It was in slow motion. Time stood still. Whit was balanced and at ease. Wingo was relaxed and confident at third base. I can still hear him saying, "We're gonna do this, Coach!"

Ping!

Wingo reacted back to third beautifully. If the right fielder had caught the ball, he was in position to tag. As the ball sailed through the air, it hit me that we were going to be the national champions. It didn't matter if the right fielder caught it or not, we were getting ready to win! Time remained still in those moments, snapshot after snapshot, as the ball dropped and Wingo touched home. Then all hell broke loose.

In athletics, it was the best feeling anyone could ever experience. All the work, all the time, all the nights away from your family. In an instant, it was all worth it. The dog pile, the hugs, the tears all seemed so surreal. It's difficult to describe because words can't do it justice. The heartfelt moments that we were experiencing were indescribable. The Gamecocks, the South Carolina Gamecocks, were national champions. To this day, we still are.

As we began to get up from the dog pile and I regained control of myself, I had one thought: I wanted to see my family. I had to go hug my wife, Jenn, and my sons, Reece and Cooper. So I immediately ran toward the stadium stairs of Rosenblatt Stadium to where they were sitting. The look on my family's face is something I will never forget. You can have all the money in the world, but that look on their faces will always be my most treasured moment. Offer me $100 million and I'd say forget it. I'd take that moment. Those who know me realize I left a place, Chapel Hill and the University of North Carolina, that I loved and in which I was deeply entrenched. My wife left a job and a boss, basketball coach Roy Williams, that she loved so dearly. I left friends that I cherished. Some of them, to this day, still can't come to grips with why I left. And, most importantly, our family left a hospital and a medical team that had helped save my little boy, Reece, from leukemia. I was overcome with emotion because all of a sudden all of that hit me. I was so thankful my son got to live, to see his daddy be part of a national championship team.

As I was walking back toward the field, I witnessed sixty-year-old men crying like babies. I've said this many times, and no one can convince me otherwise: there is not another university, city or state that this national championship could have meant more to than it did to the University of South Carolina, Columbia and the state of South Carolina. It was an honor and a gift from the good Lord that I was able to be a part of it, and it is something that my family and I will treasure for the rest of our lives. Still, let's all try to keep this accomplishment in perspective. Like we told some of our players after the game, "Don't let this be the moment that defines the rest of your lives. You will have more meaningful moments in your future, and you can do so much more for society than winning this championship. Our coaching staff all thinks that being the best dad, best husband, best friend is far more important than allowing this to define who you are." That was our message. I have no doubts that our players got it.

One of the main reasons they got it was because they had the opportunity to get to know the Teal family. Rob, Risha, Bridges and, most importantly, Bayler helped our players keep things in perspective. I will go to my grave knowing the Teal family helped our players in the national championship. The picture of Rob Teal and our players holding the trophy over their heads is an image I will never forget.

Enjoy this journey that Travis Haney will take you on with the 2010 national champion Gamecocks. You will see, firsthand, that it was a colorful group, a bunch of crazy characters who really enjoyed one another. It was a group that, no matter what, always felt like it was going to win. When they stepped on the field, that's what they cared about. It was a selfless group, a true team. The most talented? Probably not. The best team? Yes!

As a Gamecock fan, this is a journey that you will be able to forever hold close to your heart.

Chad Holbrook
South Carolina associate head coach, 2008–present

FEELING VICTORY

JUNE 29, 2010

This was new.

So many seasons in the University of South Carolina's one-hundred-plus-year athletic history had ended in heartbreak of varying degrees. The school's baseball team was no different. The Gamecocks had been to the College World Series in Omaha, Nebraska, eight times before 2010. Three of those eight times, in 1975, 1977 and 2002, they had reached the national championship game only to fall. In those seasons, they were a single victory from a title. Just getting to Omaha had proven to be a challenge after Ray Tanner took the team three consecutive times, from 2002 to 2004. South Carolina lost the deciding game of an NCAA Super Regional in 2006 and 2007, falling one victory shy of the College World Series. The Gamecocks did not even make it that far in 2008 and 2009, slipping in the Regional round of the tournament.

But they were back in Omaha in 2010. The ending? It was new, all right.

Fireworks exploded as the players piled on top of one another behind second base, where the infield dirt met the outfield grass at Rosenblatt Stadium. South Carolina, at long last, had a champion in a men's sport, a champion in a major sport. The fans were just as exuberant as the players. One coach said he saw a grown man weeping in the stands. So many, in Omaha and Columbia, took a sigh of relief a century in the making. The wait was over.

"To not have a national championship for these fans, we felt like we owed them something. These fans are too good to go this long without one," said junior outfielder Whit Merrifield, who registered the title-winning hit against UCLA on June 29, minutes before midnight back in South Carolina. "After winning it, and seeing the gratitude, we understood that they needed it more than we did. People come up to me and say they've been a Gamecock fan since 1950 and that they never thought they'd see a national championship. Knowing we helped them to have this in their life, that's amazing."

A national championship, won in any way, would be special. The unique qualities of South Carolina's in 2010, however, make the story transcendent of mere athletic achievement. It was about quirky teammates who cared about one another, dominant pitching from unlikely sources, a flair for the dramatic hit and powerful inspiration that became divine along the way.

Several Gamecocks first met Bayler Teal in October 2008. A month earlier, the five-year-old Bishopville, South Carolina native was diagnosed with neuroblastoma, a form of childhood cancer that kills one-third of those it attacks. Bayler and his family gave it everything they had, but he lost his battle. He died June 24, in the midst of South Carolina's improbable run through the College World Series. The Gamecocks were already playing for him. After his death, they played in remembrance of him. The timing so seemingly supernatural, South Carolina remains convinced that Teal had a hand, and maybe more, in the school's first meaningful championship.

"We were playing for a school, playing for a state, but we were also playing for a little man that loved his Gamecocks," said assistant coach Chad Holbrook, who initially reached out to connect the team to the Teal family. "He loved our team more than most. It helped us win. I'll go to my grave knowing that young man's life made a difference in our winning the national championship."

This is the story of a little boy and a team that refused to give in or give up. Bayler lost his life, but his team won a championship. Today, both are still celebrating.

Chapter 1
FINDING SPIRIT

JUNE 4, 2010

P eek inside the coaches' locker room at Carolina Stadium, but do so at
your own risk.

There you find Ray Tanner in one of his more animated moments. South
Carolina's longtime baseball coach, in this instant, is something just this side
of the tightly wound movie managers from *Major League* and *Bull Durham*,
stalking around the room. He's yelling at everyone and no one, all at the
same time. It's a rant that's been boiling, bubbling to the surface, for weeks.
And it's spilling out here and now, in a weather delay during the Gamecocks'
NCAA Tournament–opening game against Bucknell—what might be the
worst team in the entire sixty-four-team field. (It was one of two teams in the
tourney with a losing record.)

Tanner's team is down 1–0 in the fourth inning against the Bison from
Lewisburg, Pennsylvania, a place most of the 6,712 people in the stands
could not even begin to locate on a map. It's forgivable, considering it
isn't exactly the cradle of college baseball. That's much closer to here, to
Columbia, where it is South Carolina's first postseason game at Carolina
Stadium, the two-year-old, $36.5 million structure that resembles nothing
short of a Double-A ballpark. It's far from the program's first postseason
game, however. Guided by Tanner, the Gamecocks have been in the NCAA's
eleven consecutive seasons.

So, it's perfectly understandable why Tanner is thundering around more
loudly than the storm delaying the game.

It's a good team Tanner is fielding in his fourteenth season at South Carolina, but it hasn't played like one in weeks. Losers in four of the past five games, the offense has particularly been scuffling. The Gamecocks are running out of time. Lose to Bucknell tonight, and they will have to win four games in three days, likely against the Regional's top two seeds, Virginia Tech and The Citadel, to advance. There is a panic setting in that, with a whimper, a seventh consecutive year will pass without South Carolina returning to Omaha and the College World Series, where it has previously played eight times.

It's clearly more than enough to send the fifty-two-year-old Tanner into the foulest of funks.

After he is done with his rampage to the staff—assistants Mark Calvi, Sammy Esposito and Chad Holbrook—he slams the heck out of the locker room door. Holbrook has been around two seasons, but that is long enough to know this sort of thing with Tanner is semi-regular. Holbrook manages to stay calm through the tirade—until Tanner's door slam. That sets him off. The lighthearted, affable Holbrook jumps up, opens the door and flings it closed himself.

"See," Holbrook shouts, "I can slam the door, too!"

Peek inside the team's locker room at Carolina Stadium, but do so at your own risk.

There you find the players in one of their more animated moments.

They are in the dark. A flashlight clicks on. Then another. A few cellphones then go into the air, working to light the air ever so slightly and eerily. The Gamecocks then burst into a chant. It's gibberish. They're moving and swaying around the room, which is bereft of order—and light. Some are locked arm in arm. Others are on the ground, acting as if they are bowing and praying before some sort of pagan god.

It's a chaotic scene. Just ask Calvi, who ducks his head in to look for starting pitcher Sam Dyson. He doesn't find Dyson, but he does lay eyes on a perplexing picture of his players. Calvi, confused, asks no questions and quickly closes the door.

South Carolina's baseball team, in the middle of an NCAA Tournament game it is currently losing to Bucknell—a team with a 25-33 record that backed into the Columbia Regional by winning the Patriot League tournament—is acting out the movie *Avatar*.

Yes, this is seriously happening.

The Gamecocks believe this is the solution to all that ails them. They think, with some certainty, that a séance based on a bunch of fictitious, animated blue people in a James Cameron movie is going to change the fact that they are being shut out by Bucknell and have scored one run in the past twenty-one innings.

"We were being idiots," second baseman Scott Wingo said.

Who are these clowns, exactly? Some of the dancers and prancers are asking themselves the same question. How have things gotten to this point, where natural goofballs have converted straight-faced and straight-laced seamheads into goofballs? The infirm are running the asylum.

The most certifiable of the bunch is sophomore pitcher Michael Roth. If it makes you laugh until you cry, Roth is playing comedian. If it forces you to smirk and shake your head in disbelief, Roth is behind it. And the *Avatar* reenactment has Roth's prints all over it. He's the principal reason a bunch of college kids in baseball uniforms are acting out a tribal ritual from the year's biggest blockbuster.

"We would just say and do stupid stuff all the time," Roth said.

This snapshot, though, tops the list. Their coach is hollering down the hallway. They're losing to a terrible team. And they're dancing and chanting around a dark locker room?

Meet the 2010 Gamecocks, goofy as they are good.

Bad news: the *Avatar* trick did not immediately work. Bucknell, which did not dabble in amateur theater during the delay, pushed its lead to 5–1 through five and a half innings. The South Carolina dugout was starting to look a lot more like Tanner's locker room than the players' clubhouse.

"I felt as much tension as I'd ever felt as a coach," said Holbrook, who joined the staff in 2008, following a successful run at his alma mater, the University of North Carolina. "I didn't know how we were going to get out of it. And I didn't know what to say or do to get out of it. I thought, 'Yeah, we should be able to score the four runs to tie this thing, but can we score five to win?' That crept in my mind. That wasn't a good feeling. We didn't want the players to see what we felt. We tried to do our best poker face."

The players knew, though, because they felt the same way. As the pressure built in every Gamecock's brain, first-year outfielder Robert Beary felt compelled to do something. He grabbed a bat. Then he grabbed a baseball. Then he grabbed a roll of tape and attached the ball to the bat. If the locker room séance was the cake, this ridiculous-looking, hastily crafted object was the icing necessary to complete the rally recipe.

Beary galloped around the dugout, yapping at every player to touch the bat and latch on to a rather simple baseball concept that had somehow escaped a team that won forty-three games in the regular season: put the bat on the ball. Beary, a junior college transfer from Florida, even wrote those words at the top of the fungo, which coaches use to hit grounders during infield practice.

"It should look like this!" he barked at them, pointing emphatically at the ball, snugly taped to the bat's sweet spot.

The team broke out into laughter, reverting to the looseness of its rain (delay) dance mode. Beary unknowingly had constructed the Gamecocks' postseason mascot. He had made something the team would come to fully believe was enchanted, even if it was not completely understood at the time of its birth.

"I think a lot of people," Wingo said, "were like, 'What the crap's he doing?'"

Beary and another reserve, senior Jeff Jones, started messing with the bat, which they called the "Avatar Spirit Stick." They began to experiment with its potential power. They started pointing it in various directions. And, believe it or not, the actual ball seemed to obey the stick's holder. If Beary pointed it toward left field, say, someone would fly out to the left fielder. If Jones aimed it down and toward second base, someone would ground out to second.

Getting a bit adventurous in the sixth inning, Beary and Jones pointed the bat toward the night sky—"to get a little backspin," they said. Freshman outfielder Evan Marzilli, thrust into the lineup by Tanner after playing sparingly during the season, hit a two-run home run to cut Bucknell's lead to 5–3. It was Marzilli's ninth start of the year and his first time to hit in the leadoff spot since the opening weekend of the season, back in February. It was just Marzilli's third home run of the year. The homer launched South Carolina back in the game, and it turned the Gamecocks into spirit stick believers.

"We looked at each other like, 'No way,'" Beary said.

A problem arose in the eighth inning, when Tanner sent the stick's creator into right field as a defensive replacement. With Beary actually in the game, who would be its keeper? Beary turned to freshman pitcher Patrick Sullivan, a seldom-used reliever from Columbia who had thrown six innings all season. Sullivan, wide-eyed, accepted the challenge.

Three pitches into the inning, Beary made a terrific diving catch in the gap on a well-struck ball by Bucknell's best hitter. If he led off with an extra-base hit, with the Bison still ahead 5–4, perhaps South Carolina would have fallen behind big, and for good. Instead, Beary's catch started a 1-2-3 inning, and the bats finally arrived in the bottom of the inning. Center fielder Jackie Bradley Jr. hit a wall-scraping two-run home run to left field to give South Carolina the lead. Third baseman Adrian Morales's three-run shot later in the inning iced the game. Roth, king of the Gamecock goofballs, pitched the final three and one-third innings perfectly to get the victory, his first of the season. Sullivan, of course, was assigned the role of permanent caretaker of the stick.

The 9–5 final looked fairly predictable and expected, but the game's dramatic, and weird, turns were hidden deep within the box score. The victory against Bucknell had rekindled the team's fire. Beginning that night, South Carolina would win eleven of twelve postseason games, including an unprecedented six in a row after dropping the opener in Omaha.

The Avatar Spirit Stick was along for the ride. In fact, as Wingo sprinted in with the run that won the national championship, Sullivan had the bat lunging for home plate. It was closer to the plate, actually, than any South Carolina player.

"It's pretty dumb when you think about it," Beary said, pausing to laugh, "but it brought the team together, so maybe it wasn't that dumb at all."

Probably not, considering the spirit stick is now hallowed by the Gamecocks just as much as the NCAA championship trophy. To them, there is no trophy without the stick. And there is no stick without Bucknell.

Chapter 2

OPENING DOORS

FEBRUARY 21, 2009

Having coached in the College World Series four times, and in the NCAA Tournament another fifteen, Ray Tanner is fairly familiar with the nervous energy that accompanies a big ballgame. Season openers often carry that same feeling, regardless of the opponent. Coaches plan and plot for months. Practice starts in the fall, and the off-season has built to this moment, when everyone gets their first chance to see what the team has.

The 2009 opener had that quality to it, but there was much more afoot. On February 21, South Carolina christened Carolina Stadium, its $35.6 million jewel of a college baseball venue. The new park—located less than a mile from its predecessor—was literally a decade in the making. Tanner recognized that the school's lovable, historically charming Sarge Frye Field was enough for the Gamecocks to compete for SEC titles and vie, every now and again, for a spot in the College World Series.

But with a newer, bigger and brighter park—most of the since-razed Sarge was colored a concrete gray hue—Tanner sensed an opportunity to move up in the college baseball world. The Gamecocks could go from very good to great. They could go from a team that reached the College World Series to one that could win it.

Every year, good high school and junior college players want to play for South Carolina. But the best, the very best, would want to play three years at a top-of-the-line facility. The stadium, too, would seat more fans and be friendlier in terms of access and sightlines. At the sunken Sarge, a rooftop down the first base line was a popular vantage point. Luxury suites, replete with food and beverages, would become the new perch. Carolina Stadium would please players and fans alike.

Tanner was dogged in his pursuit of a new home, even if it sometimes— OK, often—led to headaches. Tanner's calves were in excellent shape from all the hoop-jumping that came along with a political process that required years and years of patience and posturing. No more was that the case than when builders told Tanner he would have to wait an additional year to get into the building. The Gamecocks were to move in for the 2008 season. Tanner had promised outstanding players such as Justin Smoak, the Charleston-area native now with the Seattle Mariners, that they would be among the first to play in the new stadium. Instead, he had to break the news to them that, by no fault of his own, the promise had been broken.

In spite of the setbacks, Tanner remained unflappable, consistent in moving toward a finish line that often was not visible.

"It wasn't like his world was coming to an end when it didn't go up," said pitching coach Mark Calvi, on staff the four seasons before Carolina Stadium was finished. "There wasn't a damn thing he could've done to make the stadium appear any sooner. It was just going to make him look bad. He just moved right along."

Still, for a stretch, Tanner spent more time at the corner of Williams and Catawba, at the pile of dirt and rock that eventually became Carolina Stadium, than he did at the Sarge. Tanner's handprint was on every little facet of the new stadium. It was his. Everyone knew it. Everyone was fine with it. There was the construction crew's foreman—and then there was Ray.

Sometimes, Tanner even celebrated wins at the empty, dark site. He would mourn losses there, too. His primary focus was on the teams playing at the Sarge, of course, but his vision was always cast forward, to the day when the Gamecocks would finally play at the new building. It had been that way for the majority of Tanner's twelve seasons leading up to the stadium's debut. As the day drew nearer and nearer, Tanner's longing for it grew. He wanted to stand on that top dugout stair and coach his team from a new vantage point.

In February 2009, the day arrived. Tanner had nerves, incomparable nerves, but they were a good thing. Country star and former Hootie and the Blowfish frontman Darius Rucker, a South Carolina alum, sang the national anthem. Along with former Gamecocks coaches June Raines and Bobby Richardson, Tanner helped cut a ribbon to officially open the stadium. The late February weather cooperated. So did Duquesne, rolling over in a 13–0

Gamecocks victory that featured a one-hitter by starter Sam Dyson and two other South Carolina pitchers.

"I'd say it was perfect," Dyson said of the day, following his five shutout innings, "except for that hit."

No one complained, though, as they exited Carolina Stadium's gates.

With a new stadium came a new level of expectation. That word—expectation—is a highly intriguing one at South Carolina, where fans are more demanding than at the majority of schools across the country.

Take assistant Chad Holbrook's former coaching stop, North Carolina. The basketball team, of course, is king. If the UNC baseball team—a traditionally strong program, in its own right—does anything, it only adds to whatever the hoops team did (or did not do) in the preceding months. In the Southeastern Conference, football is the sport that drives a lot of schools that also have successful baseball programs. Louisiana State is a prime example. At most schools, baseball serves as the athletic department's icing. In cold-weather regions, it rarely provides even that much.

South Carolina is a football school, almost everyone would agree. But the program has just one conference title, the 1969 ACC championship, in its 118-year history. That the men's basketball team has not won an NCAA Tournament game since the early 1970s does not help matters, either. The results leave a success-starved fan base hungry for something positive in the springtime. The fans want a winner on the diamond every year. So much so that Tanner and his staff, and even the young athletes, hear from fans if things are not going as well as expected.

Entering 2010, the Gamecocks had not reached an NCAA Super Regional in three seasons and had not been to the College World Series since 2004. Tanner said some "supporters" reinforced the notion that the wait felt more like sixty years rather than six.

"The perception was that we hadn't been in such a long time," Tanner said. "That's OK. The reason I'm here to begin with is because of expectations in this conference for all teams that participate. At this school, there are expectations for baseball. I like that."

The opening of Carolina Stadium only turned up the thermostat on those expectations. In the weeks preceding the 2010 season, South

Carolina athletic director Eric Hyman, speaking on a Columbia radio station, said the Gamecocks should regularly be in Omaha because of the sparkling new facility.

That's one thing to think. It's another to say it in an athletic department staff meeting. It's another, entirely, to say publicly and consciously float that thought to already ravenous fans. News of Hyman's soft ultimatum quickly reached the baseball office, leading to a number of snarky jokes that masked the truth inside those walls: it hurt.

One person in the athletic department said it this way: it was no different than if an AD had been openly critical of Dean Smith or Mike Krzyzewski, of Joe Paterno or Bobby Bowden. Tanner might not have the tenures or titles that those men do, or did, but that is how it was received in the office.

Tanner and his staff already wanted to win more than anyone, and now the fans' fires had been stoked by the bossman and the new stadium.

"I want to win, regardless," Tanner said. "You could trade it with Yankee Stadium, and I'd want to win as much as I ever did."

Tanner developed that trait well before his coaching career even began.

Tanner, all five feet, nine inches of him, was not the most outstanding baseball player, but he got the absolute max out of his talent. And he was a guy that you wanted on your team—mainly because you didn't want him on the other team.

That's why Sam Esposito recruited, signed and played the Smithfield, North Carolina native on the left side of his North Carolina State infield. Esposito and Tanner got along because they were essentially the same person, separated only by age. When they didn't get along, it was because they were essentially the same person. Tanner ran out of eligibility, but he had nowhere to go, really. So he stayed on as an assistant to Esposito and, at age twenty-eight, became a very young head coach at NC State. Tanner had his own mannerisms and philosophies, sure, but he was the Peter of Esposito's disciples.

"It's one of those things where imitation is the biggest form of flattery," said Sammy Esposito, Sam's son, who joined Tanner's South Carolina staff in 2007. "When you do that about something as far as a profession, it means a lot. Now, I'd do it the same way Coach Tanner does it."

Tanner took with him Esposito's charismatic, easygoing and influential way with people off the field—and his emotional, temperamental manner on it.

"He has an addiction to win. He has a craving to win. That's what he's about," said outfielder Whit Merrifield, a junior on the 2010 team. "He's so fiery. He just wants to win, at any cost. That's the kind of player I am, so I loved playing for him. He would get in your face if you needed someone to get in your face. He would pat you on the back if you needed that, too."

Working in concert with Tanner's honesty is a refreshing approach to practice. He understands the importance of practice while also maintaining that there is such a thing as overdoing it. He sometimes asks coaches he encounters who the practice is designed for, players or coaches? Is it to help maximize players' talents, or is it to placate coaches into believing they have done their jobs?

In his three years at South Carolina, the longest practice Holbrook can recall is two hours and forty-five minutes. That, he says, would be the shortest practice at a lot of schools. The other assistants independently bring up Tanner's practice schedule. They all reason that it keeps the players in better spirits during the season—and doesn't wear them out, mentally or physically, for the stretch run and postseason.

"We do our work and we get off the field," Holbrook said.

Another Tanner trademark: let your assistants work. Tanner is no micromanager. He hires people he believes he can fully trust, and he lets them go to work. He doesn't meddle or mess with them. Tanner allows them to do radio interviews. He encourages them to seek head coaching opportunities, if that is a career goal.

As a byproduct, Tanner creates a positive office environment. Walk in any given morning and the coaches are chirping at one another, playfully joking and jabbing. They're laughing. They're smiling. And just wait until they start doing their impersonations of one another.

"Ray doesn't want to work in a miserable place, so he's not going to let it be one," Esposito said. "It's not work, ultimately. At least it doesn't feel like work. You're getting stuff done, but you're having a good time."

In short, Tanner is a good boss. There is far more to him than baseball, too. Tanner and his wife, Karen, have worked for years to help gravely ill children and the less fortunate through the Ray Tanner Foundation, which, among other things, sponsors annual 5K and 12K runs and an auction. In December 2010, Tanner was nominated for a community service award given by the United Nations for his work with impoverished men in Columbia at the Oliver Gospel Mission.

The University of South Carolina Baseball Team's Journey
to the 2010 NCAA Championship

"I knew what he was about, from afar, but it's exceeded my expectations to be in the same dugout and offices with him," Holbrook said. "He's much more than I even thought he was, as a coach and as a person. He's given so much that it's nice to see him be given the ultimate prize."

Given? No, Tanner and the Gamecocks would have to work for it.

Chapter 3
CREATING IDENTITY

MARCH 9, 2010

On the second day of the second week in March, Ray Tanner turned to his top assistant, Chad Holbrook, and said something pretty outrageous: "I was due one of these years."

South Carolina was 6-4. The season not even a month old, Tanner had already started to bag the year. As much as he was being dramatic, and prematurely negative, there was a part of him that believed what he told Holbrook.

Tanner entered 2010 thinking he had some idea of what to expect. The first ten games, though, had not offered much to comfort him about the team's direction. The Gamecocks mowed through Duquesne, a program going extinct after the season, in the opening weekend. But they showed very little spunk in dropping two of three at East Carolina, which bounced them from the 2009 NCAA tourney via a soul-sapping rally in the Regional final. The games in Greenville, North Carolina, were close, but something about the energy was off. Tanner wrestled with the idea that this team might not have "it," and particularly at the plate. Previous Tanner teams mashed the ball, regularly hitting more than one hundred home runs in a season. This one would not.

Tanner presumed his best power hitter would be Nick Ebert, who led the team with twenty-three home runs in 2009. Ebert, a JUCO product from north Florida, was a late-round selection by the New York Yankees. But he turned down the Bronx Bombers, returning to school with the hope of improving his draft stock and winning a bunch of games as a senior.

One problem: Ebert, a generally good-hearted kid who worked hard on the field, had neglected his academic work. Hung up in the appeals process, the uncertainty about his future took a toll on his swing. Despite being cleared to play by the East Carolina series, Ebert was in such a slump that Tanner was not entirely sure what to do with the first baseman who had carried the Gamecocks for lengthy stretches the previous season.

On top of that, steady and well-rounded outfielder Jackie Bradley Jr. was on the shelf. Bradley broke the hamate bone in his right hand a couple of weeks before the season began, an injury that can sometimes linger for months. The school said the best case for Bradley's return was mid-March. Even then, he would have to regain strength and confidence in the hand. Freshman Evan Marzilli, despite one of the worst fall camps the coaching staff could recall, was Bradley's replacement in the outfield.

South Carolina would lean on its pitching. It knew that going in, but Mark Calvi was still sorting out his staff in February and March. Veterans Blake Cooper and Sam Dyson were locks for weekend spots, but neither sophomore Nolan Belcher nor freshman Tyler Webb had emerged as a strong No. 3 starter. Calvi spent the entire off-season thinking John Taylor would be his closer, only to watch Taylor sputter coming out the gate. Calvi was convinced the staff's talent was there, but that fact, by itself, was not enough to settle it.

The 2010 Gamecocks, in early March, were in the heart of an identity crisis.

The idea consumed Tanner on the four-and-a-half-hour bus ride home from East Carolina. What was the deal with this team? On paper, it looked pretty good. ECU was good, too. But the Gamecocks were lifeless. Once they got down a run or two, they appeared to be in a state of shock. Where was the resilience? Where was the leadership?

These things rolled around in Tanner's mind as the bus rolled down Interstate 95, back into South Carolina. He was silent the whole way home. No player or assistant dared bother him. They let Tanner be.

"What kept coming back to me was, I knew we had a pretty good team, but there was something missing," Tanner said. "The problem I had was, I didn't know what was missing. I was trying to find it. That whole bus ride crushed me."

Tanner repeatedly told himself it would pass and that he would feel better as Columbia approached. That didn't happen. In fact, the opposite did. When the bus pulled into Carolina Stadium, Tanner ordered everyone into the locker room. He didn't know what he was going to say, and the team certainly didn't, but he figured it would spontaneously come to him.

What emerged was a speech that likely forced the stadium's maintenance crew to repaint the clubhouse walls. Even though the Gamecocks were competitive in those games at East Carolina, Tanner was not going to tolerate a dugout full of flat-liners. He would be the defibrillator, sparking the Gamecocks to life. Pulling a page from Esposito's book, Tanner went around the room and picked apart every player in it. From No. 1 starter to preseason All-SEC performer to reliever who would not pitch, no one was safe. No one.

"I basically went into the locker room to express, 'We're OK, but what we're doing, it's not good enough,'" Tanner said. "It grew into something more than that."

Freshman Christian Walker was a high school star who had read his name in the paper too many times. Junior Whit Merrifield, receiving the worst of it, was a pretty boy who never wanted to get his uniform dirty. Tanner continued down the roster, barely taking time to breathe. JUCO newcomer Adrian Morales was the only player to shoot back at Tanner, when Tanner asserted Morales had not been going to class.

If the batboy ever did something to irk Tanner, he heard about it that day.

"I probably made some of my players mad," Tanner said. "That wasn't the point. The point was to find out what was missing so we could become a better team. Sometimes, as coaches, you don't always have the best delivery. Your message might be great, but your delivery's not always great.

"I probably didn't have the best delivery that day."

Tanner's speech did little to end his team's wandering in the wilderness.

A week after the East Carolina series, the Gamecocks split the first two games of a three-game set with Clemson. The Tigers then came to Columbia and destroyed South Carolina 19–6 in the Sunday rubber game.

The University of South Carolina Baseball Team's Journey to the 2010 NCAA Championship

It was the most runs Clemson had ever scored against the Gamecocks in Columbia, and the teams have played since 1899. The Tigers hit grand slams in the first and ninth innings. A Carolina Stadium record 8,214 fans showed up—and very few were still in their seats three and a half hours later. Those who were wore orange.

Two days later, South Carolina hosted 3-9 Valparaiso in a game that, the Gamecocks hoped, would restore some confidence after their recent failures against quality non-conference opponents. When the wheels started coming off Belcher in the second inning, and Valpo took a 3–0 lead against the little lefty, Tanner leaned in to Holbrook and offered his bleak forecast for the rest of the season.

"I'd been pretty consistent over the years," said Tanner, who had made ten consecutive trips to the NCAA Tournament entering 2010. "I thought, 'This could be a challenging year. It happens. It happens.' You don't want it to, but there are a lot of outstanding coaches that have had years they'd like to forget. I guess I was somewhat guarded this was going to be one."

That thought would never cross Tanner's mind again. A ten-run third inning against Valparaiso signaled a turn in South Carolina's season. Brady Thomas had a two-run double, Morales a three-run double and Merrifield a two-run home run in the big inning that stopped Tanner's bellyaching. The Gamecocks won 12–4 and, in effect, created the imperfect but ultimately effective blueprint for several postseason wins, including that Regional rally against Bucknell. The offense would run hot and cold all season, but often it would show just when hope seemed to be fading. South Carolina's deep and diverse pitching staff could keep it in games, giving the offense every chance to—poof!—magically appear.

A key to the keep-the-score-close pitching component was Jose Mata. The side-arming right-hander got his first win against Valpo, going six innings in relief. Mata, whose delivery sank so close to the ground that it was a feat his knuckles never scraped the mound, gave up just two hits. If Belcher, Webb or another starter did not have his best stuff, Mata could pick up the game as early as the third or fourth inning. On those days, he would become a version of the third starter—without actually starting the game. A JUCO product from Miami, Mata turned down Division I scholarships to walk on at South Carolina. He made that decision because he wanted to be part of a program that won at a high level.

Beginning with that Tuesday victory against Valpo, the Gamecocks did just that in 2010. Immediately following that thirteen-run loss to Clemson, South Carolina won thirteen consecutive games. The Gamecocks went from March 9 to March 28, two series into the conference schedule, without losing a game.

In retrospect, Tanner was wrong. There was nothing missing.

"We weren't there yet," Tanner said. "We just hadn't found out who we were yet."

On the road to self-discovery, the Gamecocks also found inspiration.

Chapter 4
TACKLING MONSTERS

MARCH 13, 2010

Chad Holbrook could not watch.

The South Carolina assistant retreated to the far corner of the Carolina Stadium dugout and turned his head. When seven-year-old Bayler Teal threw out the first pitch before the Gamecocks' Saturday afternoon game against Brown, wave upon wave of emotion crashed into Holbrook. He had already seen this picture. Not quite four years earlier, while he was still a North Carolina assistant, Holbrook's son, Reece, threw out the first pitch before the Tar Heels faced North Carolina State. It was a day of celebration.

In September 2004, Reece, two years old at the time, was diagnosed with leukemia. An agonizing chapter for the Holbrooks ended when Reece went into remission, a calm that still exists today. Still, cancer evokes a feeling of terror inside Holbrook. He knows it is the invisible monster, always lurking, always present. The monster breathes, Holbrook jumps. The monster shifts, Holbrook freaks. Every headache and muscle spasm Reece complains of still sends Holbrook and his wife, Jennifer, into a panic.

"That's what cancer does," Holbrook said. "It eats at your ability to enjoy the day. It's tough to enjoy the simple things in life when you know you have a kid that could take a turn for the worst at any moment."

That's why Holbrook had to turn away from Bayler's first pitch. He might have won that day's battle, but Holbrook knew, even then, that Bayler's war would ultimately be lost. His prognosis was not a hopeful one.

Bayler learned on September 17, 2008, that he had neuroblastoma, an aggressive form of pediatric cancer that often inflicts the abdomen before spreading elsewhere. By the time the third most common childhood cancer was detected in Bayler, five at the time, it had moved to his bone marrow and lymph nodes. Ron Neuberg, the doctor who diagnosed him, gave Bayler a 30 percent chance of beating it.

Bayler spent the next month at Palmetto Health Children's Hospital in Columbia, forty-five minutes from the Teals' home in Bishopville. South Carolina's football team came for a visit in late October. So did the baseball team, thanks to Graham Couch, a Bishopville native who was then a part of the team. Several players and coaches entered Bayler's hospital room expecting to see a bedridden, sickly boy who could barely open his eyes or raise his head off the pillow. Instead, Bayler was smiling. He was laughing. He was jumping on the couch. Surely they had come to the wrong room. They were looking for Bayler Teal, a five-year-old with cancer. Who was this kid?

There was no way they could have known how the story would play out, but this was the Gamecocks' formal introduction to Bayler's spirit. It was the first time they encountered a little boy who could fight his fanny off—and somehow manage to have a terrific time doing it.

Everyone who came into contact with Bayler had trouble believing he was actually sick. He would challenge his doctors to pretend fights. Laughing, they would play along. They even started to initiate them with Bayler.

"Wanna fight?" Neuberg would ask him, smiling.

"Get married!" Bayler would fire back. "Join the army!"

Quite the prankster, when nurses would come to check on him, Bayler adeptly used a sound-effect machine in his hospital room. Fart sounds were its specialty. The nurses, appalled but amused, would gasp.

"Bayyyyyyyyler," they would say, feigning indignation, as he would giggle himself into a fit before showing them the gag.

Bayler's parents, Rob and Risha, were shut out of the room where his first radiation treatment took place because of the potentially harmful rays emitted. From an adjacent room, they were able to watch a small monitor to see if he was OK. As they watched, they noticed his lips were moving.

"What's he doing?" Rob wondered.

"Is he singing?" Risha said.

They leaned toward the screen until they could faintly hear Bayler singing "Awesome God," a popular Christian song. It was on repeat in Bayler's brain. He was grinning.

"That boy loved some church," Rob said.

During Sunday morning sermons, the pastor at Savannah Advent Christian Church in Bishopville would sometimes spontaneously drop in this phrase: "God is good." The congregation would then respond, "All the time." Bayler thoroughly enjoyed that act of participation. More than anything, he loved having permission to yell something in the middle of church. But the kid Neuberg called "a little evangelist" also practiced his preaching.

Soon after his diagnosis, Bayler told his parents that Jesus sat on the edge of his bed and told him everything was going to be OK. This was not the product of an overactive childhood imagination. With every healthy and sick cell inside him, Bayler firmly believed in Jesus.

After his first hospital stay ended, in November 2008, Bayler and his family returned to church. The pastor, following the tradition, said, "God is good." His voice audible over everyone, Bayler shouted, "All the time!"

The congregation froze. Some smiled. Others bawled. Everyone received the message: a little boy was showing to-the-core faith, more than most of them had in their adult lives. He did so even as he faced adversity that would one day kill him. Cancer would take his life. His heart and soul would remain untouched.

On the Gamecocks' initial hospital visit, Holbrook pulled Bayler's dad aside. He asked for Teal's cellphone. Confused, Teal handed it to him and watched as Holbrook punched his number into it. Holbrook, then thirty-seven, told Teal, twenty-seven, to call anytime he had a question—or if he just wanted to talk.

"You can call me at two o'clock in the morning," Holbrook said. "Seriously."

Two weeks later, Holbrook called Teal. He let him know the baseball team was "adopting" the family for Christmas. The Teals, facing piles of medical bills, received about $1,000 from the team. They used some of the money to buy gifts for Bayler's brother, Bridges, who was two years younger. But most of it went to Bayler, who turned six on that Christmas Eve. The highlight for Bayler was an electric motorcycle. It was a thrill just before his battle resumed in the new year.

In January 2009, the family went to Medical University of South Carolina Hospital in Charleston for additional chemotherapy and stem cell treatments. There, Bayler encountered "Red Devil" chemo. It's three or four times stronger than most chemo treatments—and probably ten times stronger for someone as young and small as Bayler. Doctors told Rob and Risha that the medicine made adults wish they were dead. It is so potent that it makes the stem cells necessary. They are needed to replenish what is laid to waste by the chemo.

Bayler eventually made it through that stretch, feeling strong enough for a Disney World trip in May. With Bayler relatively well, the Teals say it is one of their favorite memories. In the summer, Bayler underwent antibody treatments in an effort to prevent recurrence. It was positive to be in that treatment phase, but it was physically rough on him.

On September 19, 2009, one year after the diagnosis, the Teals had an "End of Treatment Party." They felt confident Bayler had beaten cancer.

In a checkup the next week, though, Neuberg noticed something unusual with Bayler's right eye. It concerned him, and for good reason. By the first of October, not even two weeks after his party, the Teals learned that Bayler had a tumor in his brain and another on his spine. Cancer's respite was a short one. Its return caused Neuberg to start thinking more realistically. The initial survival odds sink dramatically for kids who do not kick the disease on the first try. Neuberg knew that. The thought pierced him, too, because Bayler had become one of the favorites around the clinic.

For those in healthcare, there are emotions evoked every time a sick child enters the hospital's doors—Neuberg said it will be time to retire when that is not the case any longer—but Bayler was different. He was not bitter. He looked forward to coming in and hated leaving. Even when toxic medicine was flowing into and through his body, he continued to light up the room.

"I wouldn't share him. He was mine," said Kimberly Boland, whom Rob and Risha wholeheartedly agree was Bayler's favorite nurse at the hospital. "He was just always happy. He had a spirit about him that was completely different than the kids we see."

His family and friends always said Bayler had an "old soul." He preferred to hang out with adults and converse rather than play. He didn't particularly enjoy cartoons.

The University of South Carolina Baseball Team's Journey to the 2010 NCAA Championship

Really, who was this boy? And why in the world did this child have to be the one stricken with such an illness? Could he have been a congressman? A doctor? A preacher? A movie star? What could he have done in his life without such a sentence?

"You don't want to say he was special, because you feel biased," Rob said, "but he was."

Bayler had brain surgery in October 2009 to remove the tumor and then followed with more radiation. By December, though, he was again doing poorly. Cancerous areas had appeared in his knee and shoulder. Neuberg pulled the family into a small space on the hospital's fifth floor known as the "bad news room."

No bigger than a walk-in closet, just stepping inside it seems to filter out all color from the world. And yet it is where some of the strongest emotions are displayed. There, Neuberg told two young parents that things were about to get much, much tougher. Bayler's blood cell and hemoglobin counts, powerless against the raging disease, were not bouncing back. His body had essentially learned how to spit out the medicine it was administered.

Bayler was still in the midst of that uphill trek when he threw out the first pitch in March 2010, a few months later. He strode to the Carolina Stadium mound that day like a warrior. Bayler Teal, tough as steel. That is what one family friend always said about him. Bayler was going toe to toe with cancer. What was throwing a baseball?

That thought reached the South Carolina dugout, too.

"Even when he was at his sickest, you never got the impression that he felt like he was dealt a bad hand," Holbrook said. "He always had a way of giving you energy and giving our players energy. You never got a feeling that he felt sorry for himself. It was certainly his right. He had every right to feel down. The way he handled it, the way he was around our team, was awfully inspiring. He just kept keeping on."

Chapter 5
SOLVING PUZZLES

MARCH 27, 2010

Fairly typical of Sam Dyson's career at South Carolina, the outing was a struggle.

That's not to say things were going poorly for the redshirt junior with a powerful right arm, but Dyson was dancing awfully close to the flames. At any moment, the Floridian could have been torched by Auburn, the best offensive team in the Southeastern Conference. The Tigers led the nation's top-rated league in average (.348), slugging (.591), on-base percentage (.423), runs (584) and hits (816).

Not exactly the kind of team you want to repeatedly give scoring opportunities. But that's precisely what Dyson was doing in a Saturday afternoon game that would have given South Carolina thirteen consecutive victories, including five in a row to begin SEC play.

At least Dyson did not walk anyone. That's a major peeve to head coach Ray Tanner and pitching coach Mark Calvi. Dyson, though, did allow ten Auburn hits in seven innings. The Tigers had two in the first, one in the second, three in the third, two in the fourth and two more in the seventh. Still, Dyson did not allow a single run.

He had help.

The University of South Carolina Baseball Team's Journey to the 2010 NCAA Championship

Michael Roth pitched two-thirds of an inning and Matt Price got the final four outs, for his second save of the season, in South Carolina's 2–0 victory at Auburn. The bullpen provided more, though, than the last two innings of the team's shutout. While Dyson was laboring, his fellow pitchers were doing the same. Really, they might have been sweating more than the guy on the mound. In fact, it is a good thing Dyson could not sense what was going on behind him in the Plainsman Park bullpen; it might have proven distracting.

Led by the staff's polar opposites, the quirky Roth and rock-solid Jay Brown, the bullpen became the most superstitious part of a superstitious team in a superstitious sport.

"The pitching staff was definitely the goofiest part of any team I've ever been on," Roth said. "If you looked out in that bullpen, we were having a blast. I think it kept a lot of the guys sane."

Sanity? Pitchers? C'mon, that's a good one. By comparison, Mark "the Bird" Fidrych would seem buttoned up against some members of South Carolina's pitching staff. The relievers would run around in circles high-fiving one another if a Gamecock hit a home run. If there were two balls and two strikes on a batter, with two outs in an inning—what is called "deuces wild" in baseball—the bullpen would work like mad to get its pitcher out of the inning. The relievers also did it if a Gamecock were at the plate, urging the team's hitters on, too.

There were different routines, each initiated and called out by Brown. There was "whiskey," in which the pitchers would shake one hand, half-cupped. It became "double whiskey," with two hands involved, if there was a foul ball. There were "lassoes," in which the bullpen would try to metaphorically rope the pitcher and bring him back to the dugout. There were others: going fishing, crazy arms, wheelchair, bow and arrow, bow and arrow with poison, bow and arrow with fire. Sound crazy enough yet?

"We kind of made them up as we went," Brown said.

At one point, the pitchers were "shooting" chewed-up bubble gum–tipped "arrows" from their "bows."

The activities became so entrenched and serious that pitchers Jimmy Revan and John Taylor tinkered to come up with a spreadsheet. Stats had to be established. Trends had to be followed. The superstition had measures of science in it. The routines that statistically worked were kept. Ones that did not were scrapped. In the players' minds, the "deuces" actions were key ingredients in winning.

"Our whole team seriously believed in it," Roth said. "We'd say, 'OK, let's give the pitcher some help with this.'"

The Gamecocks' pitchers were not just bizarre; they were good. They weren't great, individually. There were no lights-out, first-round-type arms on the staff, from Friday night starter to closer. But, together, Calvi, the forty-one-year-old in his sixth season as the team's pitching coach, saw something that made him believe there was potential for collective success.

Calvi says every season is like a puzzle with the pieces scattered all over a table. In his first five seasons with the Gamecocks, some of which were fairly successful in terms of final records, Calvi worked the puzzle together only to realize it was incomplete.

Regardless of how he reworked things—adding and removing, adapting and adjusting—there were missing pieces. He did not realize it until it was too late, well into the season. College teams are not afforded the opportunity to add players midseason, like professional teams do through trades, call-ups and signings. In college, a coach cannot redesign the picture as he goes. Negative events, injuries and suspensions are the only ways teams change.

Calvi's first South Carolina pitching staff, in 2005, included just two primary starters, Aaron Rawl and Zac McCamie. However, both had sub-4 earned-run averages. He had a closer, Brent Marsh, who saved a respectable eleven games. That staff had a 3.78 ERA, an extremely strong start in the SEC for Calvi. The subsequent four teams, though, only had one ERA under 4, a 3.93 in 2007. The 2009 staff had a 5.07 ERA. Those are not horrific numbers. They would not prevent a team from winning, necessarily. But with those stats, pitching more than likely would not carry a team, either.

Even the pieced-together 2007 staff featured six different starting pitchers and two closers. Calvi had nothing to resemble a consistent closer after Marsh. The middle-inning guys were even more inconsistent.

"I always felt he was a great pitching coach," Tanner said. "A few years ago, when our numbers weren't quite as good, we just didn't perform. We didn't have the pitchers to perform."

All the while, Calvi was getting crushed by fans. His teams had lost plenty of games before, but this was the first time he had been under the microscope. Message board threads on South Carolina's fan websites— "Fire Calvi!"—regularly appeared. Most schools' fans could not even name their pitching coach. In Columbia, they knew Calvi enough to know they wanted him gone.

"Every move you made was analyzed and criticized and out there for everyone to see it," Calvi said. "It's not like I needed to get better as a coach, or work harder. That wasn't it at all. I knew what the issues were. Until we fixed them, I was going to be the guy."

By that, Calvi meant fall guy.

Just like players, coaches have to learn and mature as they go. Calvi's recruiting philosophy, for as long as he could recall, was to bring in the best players. That sounds like the way to recruit, doesn't it? In a sense, it is. But Calvi wasn't paying enough attention to the team as a whole. He was recruiting good players but not factoring in the overall complexion of the team.

With each postseason loss for the Gamecocks—they fell on the road in the Super Regionals in 2006 and 2007 and on the road in the Regionals in 2008 and 2009—Calvi felt something shifting in his way of thinking. He was also in a position to do something about it, with the departure of lead recruiter Jim Toman, who left in 2007 to become the head coach at Liberty.

Calvi was the only coach out full time on the road. It was exhausting, but it gave him a lot of control in terms of who the Gamecocks were evaluating and eventually signing. The same thing happened the following summer. Monte Lee, promoted to a full-time assistant after Toman's departure, left to take the head job at College of Charleston. Before Chad Holbrook came on board in the summer of 2008, Calvi was again doing the heavy lifting on the road. He reeled in incredibly important position players, such as outfielder Jackie Bradley Jr., but he also worked overtime to retool the pitching staff.

Even as he recruited, the frustration continued to build inside Calvi—until the ultimate boiling point: with just two proven bullpen options in the 2009 Regional at East Carolina, both of them fatigued by June, the Gamecocks could not hold a three-run lead in the ninth inning. And they lost the Regional final.

"The bottom line is, we didn't have enough," Calvi said. "I knew help was on its way; it just wasn't there yet."

Calvi went to Tanner soon after the team returned home and told him things were about to change. He wanted to use more pitchers in each game. As a result, the Gamecocks would use more pitchers in a season. Like in the Majors, he wanted to rely on matchups—left-handers to face left-handed hitters and right-handers to face right-handed batters—instead of leaning on the same five or so pitchers all season, taxing them to the point of breakdown by the postseason.

He was committed to the idea through fall camp and into the start of 2010. For the first time, really, Calvi felt confident all the puzzle pieces were on the table. It was then a matter of locking them together, an arduous process, itself.

Calvi was convinced that side-armer John Taylor, a JUCO transfer from Florence, would be the team's closer. Taylor struggled, though, to begin the year. Calvi trained an eye on Matt Price, a gutty kid from Sumter whose fastball suddenly had zip and slider had bite. The piece fit.

The Gamecocks could not locate a third starter. They were hopeful going into the year that it would be sophomore Nolan Belcher. The lefty could not throw enough strikes. Freshman left-hander Tyler Webb, who started that 19–6 loss to Clemson, was likewise shaky. Brown, the sixth-year senior, was as dependable as could be but limited in terms of talent.

Enter Jose Mata, the submarine-style-throwing walk-on from Miami. Mata became the third starter, even though he never started a game. Mata could pick up a game early and carry the Gamecocks to their back-end relief team of Roth and Price. That piece fit, too.

During the team's thirteen-game win streak, capped by Dyson's victory at Auburn, the pitching picture came into focus.

"If you've got them, use them. What are you waiting for?" Tanner said. "We didn't have to push our pitchers to go six innings if they weren't having good games. We could make changes. Sometimes, in the past, if we put a guy out there, we had to live with it. Maybe we didn't have anything any better. That wasn't the case."

It continued the next weekend when the Gamecocks took two of three from Mississippi State and then headed to Vanderbilt on April 9 for an important three-game series in Nashville. South Carolina split the first two, sending Brown to the mound for the Sunday rubber game. The pitching captain delivered the performance of his career, throwing 6 1/3 shutout innings, two-hit ball, before turning it over to Roth and Price for the final 2 2/3 innings. Brown would not have another outing like that all season; he didn't throw a pitch after the Regional.

The Gamecocks won 2–0. It was Tanner's 1,000[th] career victory. South Carolina could not have won the series, though, without a victory two days earlier. No. 1,000 would have had to wait.

A lot of things would not have happened in 2010 without Blake Cooper.

Chapter 6

SLINGING STONES

APRIL 16, 2010

One kid stood six feet, five inches, weighed 230 pounds, threw with his left hand and had a terribly strange last name. Another kid stood five feet, nine inches, weighed 175 pounds, threw with his right hand and had a terribly average last name.

The sound of the first kid's name made the second one react, physically. He had heard it so much that week that it caused an instant, visual response. Everything inside him immediately tensed. His jaw locked. His eyes narrowed. South Carolina senior Blake Cooper became mad at the mere uttering of three syllables that were on a loop the third week in April.

"It's all you'd hear," Cooper said. "Pomeranz, Pomeranz, Pomeranz."

No hyperbole, Ole Miss's Drew Pomeranz was the college equivalent of Randy Johnson. Pomeranz's fastball regularly hit ninety-five to ninety-seven miles an hour, and the southpaw paired the heater with a devastating knuckle-curve pitch that few college kids even dream of developing. Most are happy to get their fastball consistently over the plate. Maybe a curve or a slider that sometimes works, depending on the day. But not this thing that Pomeranz was wielding. He was the real deal, as evidenced by the fact that he wound up the No. 5 overall pick in the 2010 draft, receiving the highest signing bonus ($2.65 million) of any college pitcher in the draft's history.

Then there was Cooper, the roundish, rosy-cheeked native of Neeses. Where's that? It's a question that could stump even lifelong South Carolinians. About forty miles south of Columbia, Neeses (pop. 313) features one stoplight, one grocery store nicknamed the "giant" because it serves as the hub of civilization—and little else.

"You better like Chinese or know how to cook," Cooper said, "or you're not eating."

Cooper was not even on Mark Calvi and South Carolina's radar until Cooper started playing for a traveling team called the Pendleton Cardinals. No, it wasn't based in Pendleton, South Carolina. It was run by Terry Pendleton, the 1991 National League MVP and former Atlanta Braves hitting coach.

The Pendleton Cardinals were playing in Atlanta once when the Gamecocks were on hand to scout. Cooper's coach, Tommy Dunbar, a former Texas Rangers first-round pick from Graniteville, South Carolina, grabbed Cooper before the game. He told him the coaches from South Carolina, the school Cooper grew up rooting for, thought he was going to get knocked around.

Jim Toman, then South Carolina's lead assistant, once told Cooper during the recruiting process that he could probably pitch for the Gamecocks but he had a better chance to stand out at a Southern Conference school. That chapped Cooper. He dominated the other travel team in a 1–0 victory. The opposing pitcher skipped college and was a second-round pick in the draft that year. Cooper had to become a giant-killer just to get to South Carolina. And the Gamecocks loved that about him. It's the biggest reason they took a shot on him. Calvi figured he could teach Cooper how to pitch but he could not coach heart. For all the things Cooper lacked, and there were plenty physically, drive was not one.

The baseball field was one thing. Moving from Neeses to Columbia was another. Cooper arrived on campus to awe. Doe-eyed, he would look at Calvi and say, "Coach, I don't know about all this city life." "He thought this was a big city," said Calvi, who has lived most of his life in Miami.

Cooper had freshman classes at South Carolina with as many people as there were in the hometown he had left behind. "See, I thought my high school was big until I got here," said Cooper, who graduated from Edisto High with about two hundred others. "I had trouble finding my classes in high school. I got here and was like, 'Dang.'"

The transition to college ball did not turn out to be much easier. Cooper's ERA in his first fall camp was somewhere in the neighborhood of 20.

Somehow, Cooper got himself together enough in the spring to be a reliever who got a little work to begin the 2007 season. He had logged about eight relief innings when the team's Friday night starter, Harris Honeycutt, went down with an injury.

With few options, Tanner turned to Cooper. Tanner had been particularly hard on Cooper since he arrived. When Cooper stood on the bump to make his first start, he suddenly understood why. Tanner knew he might need him immediately. He was instilling toughness in the youngster. It worked, too.

Nervous but not showing it, what would become his trademark, Cooper did not give up an earned run in five innings. He struck out six. More importantly, Cooper earned additional chances. He started eleven games as a freshman, going 7-2 to earn Freshman All-America honors from *Collegiate Baseball*. But he had that sterling record despite a 4.48 ERA, often riding the team's offense to victories.

Cooper would have one good outing and then two miserable ones. Inconsistency was a trend that continued into his sophomore (5-6, 3.94 ERA) and junior (9-4, 4.50 ERA) seasons. He could be dominant. He could be bad. Calvi's attitude: show up to the park and see which Cooper took the mound.

Sometimes, though, it was predictable which Cooper would appear. If a lineup was stacked with left-handed hitters, Cooper was in big trouble. He had developed enough pitches and control to handle hitters from the right side, but forget it when it came to left-handers. In his first three seasons, left-handed batters hit .330 against Cooper, compared to .249 for right-handed hitters.

Like Calvi, Cooper reached his last straw by the East Carolina Regional in 2009, the end of his junior season. He was done with mediocrity, he thought to himself. He was done being considered a so-called SoCon pitcher by his coaches. Cooper set out to do something lofty. He was pretty good, but he didn't desire to be good. He didn't want to be great. He wanted to be the best.

"He was doing OK. I think he got tired of just doing OK," Calvi said. "He went from this little small-town guy to wanting to be the guy the team revolves around. That was a great thing to watch."

It's one thing to say it. It's another to do it, putting in the work to go from pretty good to the school's pitching pantheon. Billy Anderson was more than willing to accommodate the request. With nearly a decade as the baseball team's strength and conditioning coach, Anderson got twenty pounds off Cooper by the end of 2009. Cooper did the work. "He got after it as hard as anybody I've seen get after it," said Jay Brown, the pitching staff's senior captain.

As he lost the weight, Cooper found a slider. Calvi had been working for more than a year with Cooper on a pitch to get lefties. The cutter, or slider, was that pitch, but Cooper just could not master it. It was a confidence issue. Cooper even admitted that.

Calvi was on a recruiting trip when he called Sammy Esposito, another Gamecocks assistant, to see how things were going in fall scrimmages. He asked how Coop had thrown that day.

"He's got a cutter now," Esposito told Calvi.

"No, he doesn't," Calvi said, flatly. "Blake can't throw a cutter."

"He can now," Esposito said.

Cooper remembers that day. He faced most of South Carolina's 2010 starters, including left-handed-hitting Jackie Bradley Jr. With a seventy-five-pitch limit, Cooper struck out eight in five innings.

Entering the 2010 season, Calvi and Ray Tanner raved that they had never seen Cooper throw this well. He had command of four or five pitches, and for a change, left-handers were getting outs rather than hits against him. He hadn't turned himself into Kip Bouknight, the best pitcher in school history, just yet. But they thought he had a shot to be that kind of force. He was throwing that well.

Cooper carried his determination into the season. Like that day back in Atlanta, with South Carolina's coaches looking on, Cooper was often fueled by the fact that he was going against the opposing team's ace. And typically, that ace looked a heck of a lot better on paper than Cooper.

"Blake Cooper used that," Gamecocks assistant Chad Holbrook said. "He used it every day."

Holbrook included, South Carolina's coaches knew exactly how to locate, and lay on top of, that button. They knew how to rattle Cooper's cage just before they released him to take the mound. They had done it since he arrived on campus—before he did, really, going back to the Pendleton Cardinals.

The University of South Carolina Baseball Team's Journey to the 2010 NCAA Championship

"Hey, you're going against a first-rounder tonight," Tanner would sometimes say to Cooper, jabbing away. "Think you can handle him, SoCon guy?"

Tanner would laugh. Cooper would not.

Pomeranz, the college pitcher prototype, was the finest example of that David v. Goliath. A better set of skills could not be constructed in a science lab. He was size, velocity and guile.

On that April evening at Carolina Stadium, Pomeranz was on. He walked four but gave up just two hits—two bunt singles—in seven scoreless innings. The Gamecocks had no idea how to attack him. It was vintage Pomeranz.

But Cooper was better.

He tossed the finest game by a South Carolina pitcher in the better part of a decade. Cooper threw the first complete-game shutout by a Gamecock since Aaron Rawl in 2006. He gave up four hits and a walk and struck out ten.

"I told our guys before the game that Blake Cooper would give us a chance," Tanner said afterward. "He was going to keep us in the game. It was going to be a close one and somehow we figured out a way to win. I can't say enough about Cooper's outing; it was extremely special."

Outdueling Pomeranz moved Cooper to 7-0. The Gamecocks won every one of his Friday night starts in the SEC until a 3–2 loss to Florida in the last regular-season series. Cooper was 10-0 until getting saddled with the loss in that one, even though he gave up three runs in 6 1/3 innings, still keeping the Gamecocks in it.

Just like he wanted, Cooper had gone from above average to ace. He finished the year 13-2 with a 2.76 ERA. He struck out 126 and opponents hit .223 against him, including .230 by left-handers—100 points lower than his first three seasons. Cooper was still left off everyone's All-America lists.

"He was probably the most underrated pitcher in the entire country," senior catcher Kyle Enders said. "He didn't get a whole lot of credit for what he did, especially his senior year. There's Pomeranz and those type of guys. You'll see those guys pitching in the big leagues one day. Will Blake? I don't know. I hope so. I just know he just relished the opportunity to go out there and beat those guys."

Numbers aside, the difference in Cooper was clear. He stood taller as a senior, after being sort of slumped over his first couple of years. He spoke with conviction after seasons of remaining quiet. A kid who was never, ever drafted before—even though the MLB draft has nearly fifty rounds—went in the twelfth round in 2010.

Cooper had accomplished the mission for his senior season.

"Coming in from high school, the talk was that I was OK, I was pretty good," Cooper said. "But I knew, down inside, there were other guys. There were guys who were just as good or better. I knew I had to work for it. I was 5-10, if you stretched me out, and 180 pounds and right-handed. That's not a good mix. That's something else that fueled me. I knew I was good enough."

The giant-killer still had a little Neeses left in him, though. Enders stood beside Cooper for the national anthem before each of his starts. Each time, Cooper would tell Enders he felt like vomiting.

"All I could think was, 'Man, how can you be nervous?'" Enders said. "'You're one of the best pitchers in the country.'"

He proved it against Pomeranz. And he would in Omaha.

Chapter 7

PLAYING INSPIRED

APRIL 22, 2010

S outh Carolina had no issue getting pumped to play at Auburn and Vanderbilt, two of the SEC's better teams. But how would the Gamecocks, after taking two of three from Ole Miss, motivate themselves for a weekend series at Georgia? The Bulldogs were 12-25 overall, with a 3-12 conference record. South Carolina (29-8, 11-4) was rolling, but continuing downhill can sometimes be tricky against lesser opponents, even those as down as Georgia.

On the ride to Athens, the coaches wondered what it would take to fire up the players. Upon arrival, though, Chad Holbrook knew the matter had been resolved. He gathered the players for a quick meeting before a Thursday workout at Foley Field. He told them he had spoken earlier in the day with Rob Teal. Teal called Holbrook to let him know that his son's health had deteriorated.

Bayler Teal was a little boy who had cancer. To the players, at least until that point, he was a little boy who would beat cancer. After all, Holbrook's son, Reece, had come through leukemia just fine. Why would this be any different?

The somber message from Holbrook changed everything. One by one, the players who were closest to Bayler and the Teals went to find Holbrook around the batting cage.

"How bad is it?" they asked, concerned. "Is he going to be OK?"

Holbrook was honest. He told them Bayler was dying.

"That was the first moment they realized the kid might not make it," he said.

The team quickly turned that punch to the gut into inspiration. Holbrook implored the Gamecocks to play that weekend for Bayler. He wanted them to put baseball, and all they had been given, in perspective, compared to what Bayler was enduring. They had visited Bayler in the hospital, some since October 2008. They had celebrated with him as he threw out the first pitch in mid-March. Now, like his family, the Gamecocks were beginning to acknowledge certain realities about the boy's ultimate fate. And they responded by playing in Bayler's honor.

Holbrook sent a text to Rob Teal, telling him South Carolina was dedicating that weekend to Bayler. Rob told his son. Bayler looked at him strangely. He had a difficult time believing what he was hearing.

"Playing for me?" he said. "Really?"

Bayler smiled.

A few months earlier, in January 2010, the Teals were in a new phase of their fight against neuroblastoma. The cancer had disappeared the previous summer, only to return by November. With cancerous areas in Bayler's shoulder and knee, the Teals returned to MUSC Medical Center in Charleston for a "drive-by rescue," in which Bayler's body was charged with stored stem cells from the visit a year earlier. The treatments and medicines that had been effective, though, were now futile. Cancer was in control of Bayler's body. It was rejecting the medicine.

Down, the Teals started exploring more aggressive options. After the initial diagnosis in September 2008, they had considered the best plan for Bayler. Specifically, the family weighed going to one of the country's top cancer centers, Sloan-Kettering in Manhattan, or staying in South Carolina.

Ron Neuberg, Kevin McRedmond and other physicians in Columbia assured the Teals that Bayler would get the same treatment at Palmetto Health Children's Hospital, and at MUSC, as he would in New York. And he would get it without the jarring life change of being far away from home. It would be the most sensible decision for the entire family.

The Teals tried that. They tried and tried. The start of 2010 was the end of the road with treatment in South Carolina. Rob Teal had heard something about a new antibody, something called 8H9, that might renew Bayler. Rob called the doctors at Sloan-Kettering and updated them on his son's condition. He told them he had been given little hope in Columbia.

"Don't believe that," one doctor said. "We've got stuff that works."

Emboldened by the promise of 8H9, Rob and Risha went to New York to scout the area and, more importantly, the hospital. The Teals were encouraged by what they saw and heard, and they returned the following week with Bayler. Even with the realistic straight talk from doctors in Columbia, the family had not yet surrendered.

"I was convinced he was going to get through it," Rob said.

Over the next three months, from January to March, the Teals spent equal amounts of time in New York and South Carolina. They were in New York for three weeks, back home for two, up for three, home for three, back in New York for one and so on. There was no prevailing evidence that 8H9 was curing Bayler, but at the very least, it was making him feel pretty darned good in the interim. Rob and Risha took him to a hockey game at Madison Square Garden. A sport on ice with sticks and hitting? (Wanna fight?) He loved it. Felt as if it were made for him.

When the family was home in South Carolina, Rob and Risha would take Bayler to Chuck E. Cheese once a week. They also took him to Carowinds, a theme park just south of Charlotte, to ride roller coasters. His energy was up, most of the time. There was a part of Rob and Risha that remained hopeful. But there was also a growing realism inside them. They were trying to seize as much of that time together as possible. They knew time was far from guaranteed, much less time in which Bayler felt well. They knew he could wake up the next day and his health could precipitously decline in a snap of the fingers. As a family, the Teals held on to that time with everything they had.

With the Bishopville community so familiar with the story, and so eager to help, there was always someone—and sometimes an army of people—at the Teals' home. So, in a way, New York provided a haven, a break from all the attention.

The hospital on the Upper East Side of Manhattan was certainly different. It was more of a cancer-treating assembly line, compared to the southern, personal touch of Palmetto Health Children's Hospital. Naturally, there were parts of Columbia that the Teals missed. Then again, this was about healing Bayler. But that did not happen in New York, either.

In April, Bayler's treatment cycle at Sloan-Kettering ended. The 8H9 had failed.

That's when Rob Teal reached out to Holbrook, painting a rather bleak picture. The Gamecocks responded by playing for Bayler—and they played well for him. Blake Cooper went eight innings to lead South Carolina to an 11–4 pummeling of Georgia the day after it learned about Bayler's condition.

A rainout the next day set up a double-header—a pair of seven-inning games—on that Sunday. In the first game, Sam Dyson pitched a three-hit shutout. The Gamecocks blew an early five-run lead in the second game but broke a 7–7 tie with a run in the top of the seventh to complete the sweep. Unlike Tanner's past teams, powered by the home run, South Carolina had transitioned to a team that liked to play smallball. It won that final Georgia game with a walk, a stolen base and a single up the middle.

"We always seemed to find a way. We were always picking people up," said leadoff hitter Whit Merrifield, who scored the winning run. "We weren't a great offensive team, but we got hits when we needed to and put up just enough runs to win."

Merrifield's arrival three years earlier had signaled the change in philosophies. Sluggers such as Justin Smoak and James Darnell were on the way out. Home runs were suddenly passé. Bunts and going first-to-third were en vogue for the Gamecocks, led by Merrifield, Mr. Smallball.

Tanner only needed to hear Merrifield's name to know he wanted him in a South Carolina uniform. Tanner was at North Carolina State when Whit's dad, Bill Merrifield, was at Wake Forest. The elder Merrifield was an All-American shortstop who twice won ACC player of the year. His wife, Whit's mom, played tennis at Wake.

Bill Merrifield's credentials were enough to make Tanner believe in Whit Merrifield's credentials. Tanner was prepared to sign him, sight unseen. He did eventually watch the Advance, North Carolina product, and it actually tested his convictions. Merrifield was just shy of six feet tall, a 140-pound shortstop who didn't field or run particularly well. He hit OK, but not for power. He was difficult to project on the next level.

For that reason, regardless of who Merrifield's dad was, a lot of in-state schools were not all that interested in him. Holbrook, then at North Carolina, can laugh about that now. Holbrook does not make too many recruiting mistakes. In January 2011, he was named by ESPN the No. 10 recruiter in college sports. But Holbrook labels Merrifield one of his biggest whiffs. He saw Merrifield as "a weak kid" and dismissed him, never taking into account his bloodline. He wasn't the only one.

Merrifield wasn't nearly as gifted as his father, but like Bill Merrifield, Whit exuded the attitude of a winner. He was confident. Given his skill set then, he was probably overconfident. But he made that a positive. "His belief in himself is off the charts," Holbrook said. "That's how he makes up for what he lacks physically. He believes he belongs. That's why he's the player he is."

As a freshman in 2008, Merrifield started sixty-two of sixty-three games for the Gamecocks. All of the starts were in center field, one of the game's toughest positions, even though he was recruited as a second baseman. Merrifield, hitting near the top of the order, led the star-studded lineup with twenty-six multi-hit games. His .326 average was behind only Smoak and Reese Havens, who both went in the first round that year. In the smallball department, growing in importance for the Gamecocks, Merrifield led the team with eleven stolen bases and twenty-three sacrifices.

As a sophomore, Merrifield hit .340 with eleven home runs, eight more than his freshman year. He again led the team in sacrifices (nine) and steals (fifteen). He started all sixty-three games, carrying a fourteen-game hit streak into 2010. Merrifield continued the streak for another twelve to begin the year, breaking Greg Keatley's thirty-four-year-old school record of twenty-five games.

There are always guys on teams who require constant attention and coaching. Then there are guys, like Merrifield, who can be set in motion and virtually left alone.

"We just let Whit be Whit," Holbrook said. "He knew what we wanted him to do. He always did the right thing. He was our quarterback on the field. We never worried about Whit."

Oh, and another thing about Merrifield. Since arriving on campus, he established himself as the team's heartthrob. His teammates called him "Hollywood" for his movie star looks and charm.

"Everybody loves Whit Merrifield. He's a good-looking kid who always smiles on the field," Holbrook said. "Moms love him. Girls love him. All the females in Columbia love Whit Merrifield."

Merrifield's appeal extended to kids, too. He was Bayler's favorite player.

Chapter 8

SMILING AGAIN

APRIL 25, 2010

The smile had returned.

After Jackie Bradley Jr. went 4 for 4 with a home run in the series finale at Georgia, it was back. The sophomore center fielder was again Jackie, the upbeat guy everyone expected to see in 2010.

Ray Tanner told Bradley in March that he didn't look happy. Bradley tried to say everything was all right, but his numbers betrayed him. He had four extra-base hits, two home runs and two doubles, in 107 at-bats leading into that Georgia series.

Bradley's right hand was the thing preventing that smile from reappearing. Two weeks before the start of the season, while Bradley was hitting in the cage, he felt excruciating pain in his palm. Because of the way the left-handed-hitting Bradley held the bat, he was at risk for a hamate bone injury to his right hand, his low hand on the bat.

Sure enough, that afternoon in early February, the bone broke. With the season quickly approaching, Bradley needed surgery immediately. But the team's hand specialist was out of the country. Assistant Chad Holbrook got in touch with, of all people, Vanderbilt basketball coach Kevin Stallings. Holbrook had recruited Stallings's son when Holbrook was at UNC, and he asked Stallings if there was a good hand doctor at Vanderbilt's hospital.

Holbrook made that call on a Saturday. Bradley was in Nashville consulting with specialist Douglas Weikert by Monday. The quick turnaround, and Stallings's help, got Bradley back on the field by late February, ahead of schedule. But with that sort of injury, it takes time to regain confidence in the hand's power and ability to absorb the shock of a metal bat striking a ball. Bradley was in the lineup from the season's opening weekend, taking at-bats by the second series, but he was a shell of himself and what was projected for his sophomore season.

A part of Bradley's early college experience was learning how to deal with injuries. The Virginian never had any in high school. Already, in his first two years at South Carolina, he had encountered plenty. And the hand wasn't even the most serious issue.

Alfreda Hagans refused to leave Carolina Stadium until she had met Holbrook in person. She wanted to shake hands and lock eyes with every South Carolina coach that would be her baby's caretaker for the next three or four years. She waited an hour for Holbrook to return from an errand.

After that exchange, Holbrook felt personally responsible for Bradley, or else his mother would drive down from Virginia. And Holbrook would not want that. Holbrook said he was constantly worried about Bradley, even though he seemed to be settling into college life—and college baseball—just fine. Holbrook's sense of duty only increased in the fall of 2008, when he was overseeing a group of players working out in the stadium's weight room. Bradley walked up to Holbrook, wearing a pained look on his face.

"Coach," he said, "I can't feel my fingers."

Holbrook told Bradley to hold out both arms. One looked like a twig, the other like a log.

"Jackie," Holbrook said, trying to remain calm, "you have a blood clot."

Holbrook was able to make that amateur diagnosis because the same thing had happened to a player at North Carolina. Bradley went immediately to trainer Brainard Cooper, who had Bradley at an area hospital within the hour.

"That's a life-threatening deal," Holbrook said. "You can drop dead in a heartbeat."

Bradley learned he has an extra rib that causes his blood to flow strangely. It is something he will have to monitor the rest of his life. He even had a minor scare with it in 2010, but nothing compared to the first time.

The stats from Bradley's freshman year did not seem to indicate anything was ever wrong with him. Bradley bounced back in time to start the season, and he exceeded the high expectations the coaches had for him. He hit .349 with eleven home runs and forty-six RBIs in sixty-one starts. He was every bit as steady as Whit Merrifield, batting second behind Merrifield much of the year.

Bradley was also a perfect complement to Merrifield in the Carolina outfield. In fact, leading into his sophomore season, the coaching staff flip-flopped the two, moving Bradley from right to center. The competitor in Merrifield wasn't thrilled about the switch, but it wasn't because Merrifield couldn't handle center. It was because Bradley would be better there. The coaches were right. He was.

Bradley's effortless fluidity in the field is why he stands apart—and why he was moved to center. He isn't particularly fast, but he makes up for it with vision and instincts. The second the ball pings off the aluminum bat, Bradley is already in motion. He's in position to make the play before most fans realize it's his ball to catch. By then, Bradley is casually flipping his glove up at the last second, making a tough play appear routine.

"He has the ability, when the ball's hit, to know where it's going to land," Holbrook said. "He doesn't have to watch it. It's insane. Only the great ones in the game of baseball can do that. Willie Mays did that stuff."

Holbrook still giggles about the best catch he ever saw Bradley make. It was early in the 2010 season, at East Carolina—during batting practice. A ball left a bat and went screaming for the gap. Every kid in the country lets that ball go. It's pregame warm-ups. Save it for the game, right? "He catches BP like it's a game," Holbrook said.

Holbrook saw Bradley take off for the ball, but he still assumed he had no shot. Bradley was able to pull up just shy of the wall and make the catch look easy. Holbrook asked Bradley about it later. It was one that had impressed even him.

"It's definitely not easy," Bradley said. "You just work and work at it. When I was a kid, playing catch, I would try to make all these crazy, diving catches all over the place. Now, compared to that, everything feels pretty normal to me."

Bradley's instinctive nature carries over to the plate, as well. In part, Tanner hired Holbrook because he wanted to tweak the team's general hitting philosophy. Specifically, the Gamecocks were striking out too much. Holbrook's answer was to get the players to stop thinking fastball so much, and especially with two strikes. He wanted them to look for off-speed pitches so they would not chase them. It was easier, he reasoned, to try to catch up with the fastball.

No one grasped the concept. South Carolina having traditionally been a slugger's paradise, Holbrook said it was like teaching a four corners offense to a basketball team that loved to push the ball up the court. As a freshman, Bradley was the only one to get it. Holbrook asked Bradley why he could do what the juniors and seniors could not.

"I pick up stuff quick," he told Holbrook.

He's always hungry for more, too. Bradley is a baseball sponge. Unlike an auto-pilot kind of player like Merrifield, Bradley has a desire to be coached. He wants to soak in more about the game. He has a deep love for baseball that shows in everything he does on the field.

"He's way beyond his years, from an aptitude for the sport. He's got an approach like a twenty-six-year-old big leaguer," Holbrook said. "Is he blessed with first-round talent? Probably not. But he has first-round instincts and first-round confidence. He has first-round knowledge of how to play the game."

Guess what round Bradley is projected to go in, in the 2011 draft.

The week after Georgia, a series in which Bradley had seven hits, he was wearing that dusted-off smile when he approached Holbrook.

"Coach," he said, "I'm 100 percent."

That was a day a lot of people, including Bradley, had awaited. Bradley said he never once gave up on the season, thinking he would never fully return to health in 2010. "It was a gradual process," Bradley said. It was just tough to smile through parts of that process.

South Carolina had won a bunch of games with Bradley at some other percentage. The Gamecocks were about to get a lot better with Bradley at full strength. Bradley had five hits and drove in seven runs in the team's series win against Alabama. He homered in the Friday and Sunday games, South Carolina's two victories in the set.

Bradley added two more home runs the following Wednesday against Winthrop, giving him five home runs in five games—more than doubling what he had done in the season's first two months. Bradley hit .425 (34 for 80) in the regular season's final nineteen games, beginning a hit streak May 11 that would extend well into the postseason. He carried it until the Gamecocks' final game of the season.

Despite the slow start, Bradley's .368 average was forty-one points higher than the closest regular in the lineup, first baseman Christian Walker. He tied Merrifield for the team lead in home runs, with thirteen. And he led the Gamecocks with sixty RBIs.

Jackie was Jackie again.

Chapter 9
CHANNELING TANNER

MAY 2, 2010

Assistant coach Chad Holbrook was called in as a reliever. South Carolina had just clinched an SEC series against Alabama, the Gamecocks' seventh consecutive series win to begin conference play, and Ray Tanner wasn't feeling well. So, that thrust Holbrook into the postgame media session in the Carolina Stadium interview room.

Holbrook revealed that Tanner, who had managed to get through the game from the dugout, was dealing with a bout of vertigo. Dizziness was only natural after that series, which included a 20–15 win in Sunday's rubber game. The Gamecocks needed a Brady Thomas home run in the eleventh inning to defeat Alabama on Friday, and it took nearly all of those twenty runs to push past the Tide in Sunday's deciding game.

In the postgame presser, Holbrook continued to come back to one player, again and again, as a catalyst. Holbrook did not know if he would ever mention Adrian Morales's name in that manner. In addition to the team's established offensive stars, Morales, 4 for 6 in the Sunday victory, was also developing into a regular contributor as the team's everyday third baseman.

Not bad for a kid who knew virtually nothing about South Carolina until the Gamecocks stumbled upon him.

Mark Calvi is a south Florida guy. Originally from Marco Island, on the other side of the Everglades from Miami. Went to Nova Southeastern University in Davie, between Fort Lauderdale and Miami. Spent eleven seasons as an assistant coach at Florida International University, in Miami, before becoming South Carolina's pitching coach in 2005.

The man knows the Sunshine State, and especially that neck of it. He knows Miami's swamps and sprawl. Naturally, it was part of his recruiting domain for the Gamecocks. As he would any year, Calvi spoke in 2009 with community college coaches in south Florida to see what sort of prospects they had. In his conversation with the coach at Miami-Dade Community College, Calvi brought up Morales's name. Calvi had seen Morales once before.

"I saw him in high school," Calvi said. "He wasn't good enough. He was good, but not good enough."

Still, something made Calvi ask about him.

"Every coach down there said they hated him, but they'd pick him first on their team," Calvi said. "Everybody. That was always the basis of their answer."

A grin flashed across Calvi's face when he heard that. Morales was not an outstanding hitter, runner or fielder, but he was the player in a good JUCO league whom the other coaches loathed because they wished he was in their dugout. Calvi relayed the message to Tanner, vouching for Morales to be part of the class.

"What kept coming back was 'good player, but a great winner,'" Tanner said. "That kept coming back. Now, that wasn't the words they were using. They kept saying, 'He's clutch. He's a tough kid. You don't want to play against him. You don't like him if he's on the other team.'"

Morales became a must-sign for the Gamecocks.

Growing up in a rough part of Miami, Morales said he knew little about South Carolina, as a state and a program. He didn't know the history. He sure as heck didn't grow up a fan, like Blake Cooper did. He just knew Miami and Florida's other traditional powers were not calling, and he wanted a chance to play collegiate baseball at the highest level.

"I saw it was one of the big dogs in the SEC," Morales said. "I didn't want to turn down an opportunity to come play in the SEC."

But would he actually play?

The players were beginning to mesh in the fall of 2009, rookies with the vets, but they weren't sure what to make of Morales. There haven't been too many Hispanic players on Tanner's teams over the years, so he was different in that regard. He said words funny. He was loud and gruff. He had never heard of sweet tea.

Whit Merrifield and Morales were both juniors, but Merrifield had been in the program two years. Morales walked in the door and, in some respects, behaved as if he had been at South Carolina even longer.

"He's the kind of guy that, when he comes in, you immediately hate him," Merrifield said. "You're like, 'Who is this kid? Who does he think he is?'"

Morales said he tried to suppress his innate leadership qualities. He tried to hold back while he got used to South Carolina—and it adjusted to him. But he probably didn't restrain himself as much as he thought he did.

"I hated Adrian. I hated him. I did not like him," sophomore pitcher Michael Roth said. "I didn't like the way he played. I don't know. I just wasn't a fan of him."

Freshman Greg Harrison hit Morales with a pitch every time he came up to bat against him during fall camp. Even in intrasquads, the other team couldn't stand Morales. One thing helped him fit in: the season. When it arrived, the Gamecocks, even those vehemently against him, suddenly figured out he was a great guy to have on their side.

"I loved him in the spring," Roth said.

He wanted to win. So did they. And even though they did not realize it at the time, the team needed a vocal leader. It had outstanding senior role models in captains Jay Brown and Kyle Enders, but they were both very quiet individuals. If they were going to provide some guidance, they would do it in a soothing, private way. They would pull a guy aside in the dugout or the bullpen. Merrifield and Jackie Bradley Jr. were by-example leaders. There were so many parts of their games that their peers wanted to emulate, but they were not in-your-face types.

From those JUCO reports, Calvi and Tanner knew Morales had that in him. And it slowly started to come out as situations arose. If a pitcher saw Morales coming to visit him on the mound, he might duck his head. He might wish it were Tanner instead.

"There were guys who would have to answer to him if there were some issues," Calvi said, "and they didn't want to."

As Morales's playing time increased, with every at-bat or inning in the field, so did his hold on the team.

"We were missing that guy in the clubhouse," Calvi said. "Adrian Morales was huge. We had to get that guy. He took ownership of that team, in a very short period of time. It's rare for a junior college kid to do that. Usually, they're kind of feeling their way."

Leadership skills only mean so much if you are not an everyday player, and Morales had to incrementally earn time through the middle part of the season. Tanner didn't start Morales in the first two games of an early April home series against Mississippi State, but he made Tanner regret it on that Sunday, going 2 for 4 with a two-run double and a solo home run.

Tanner plugged Morales in the lineup the next weekend at Vanderbilt. Morales promptly went 0 for 3 with a strikeout in both the Friday and Saturday games. He was 0 for 9 in the series by the time he went to the plate in the ninth inning Sunday, with the Gamecocks clinging to a 1–0 lead. Morales responded with a two-out double that drove in a crucial insurance run. He was 1 for 10 on the weekend, but the hit was a big one. Morales helped dump the water cooler on Tanner to celebrate his 1,000[th] career victory. Tanner grabbed Morales and got in his face.

"Why do you do this to me?" Tanner said, half serious and half joking. "You go 0 for 9 and then you come through with a clutch base hit, a clutch double like that? Don't do that anymore."

Morales listened. He was Mr. Clutch through the stretch that followed, digging his heels in to keep that starting job at third base and his spot in the heart of the order. Those roles remained his.

"I told Tanner that," Morales said. "I told him, 'As soon as I get back on the field, you're not going to take me out.'"

In Cooper's victory against Drew Pomeranz and Ole Miss, it was a 1–0 game until Morales had a three-run, bases-clearing double in the bottom of the eighth. The next weekend, at Georgia, Morales went 6 for 11 with five runs scored and five RBIs. He homered in each game of Sunday's doubleheader. The strong weekend against Alabama followed.

Morales led the team in RBIs most of the year, finishing second behind only Bradley. He led the Gamecocks with fifteen doubles, many of which plated important runs late in games. Merrifield said the team started calling Morales "Geico, because he always provided insurance."

"He's better when the pressure's the greatest," Tanner said. "You know, there are a lot of players you can't find when the game's on the line. He wants to be in there."

Again, that's different for a first-year player in a top-tier program.

"But, you know, when you go back," Tanner said, "the things Calvi heard when he was recruiting him, it all comes into focus."

Good luck comparing Morales to another player on the team. In fact, the best comparison, one that draws laughter from both men, is to Tanner. Several players assert that Morales is a mini-me of the coach.

"I like the way Tanner is," Morales said. "He's blunt about everything. He's straight-forward. He will not sugarcoat anything. He tells you like it is. I'm a grown man. I'm twenty-one, already. He's a grown man. I feel like I'm going to respect him; he's going to respect me."

Sure enough, other teams came to dislike Morales. And the Gamecocks fell in love with him.

"Look at him," Calvi said. "He's five foot seven. But he is who he is. He's the Tasmanian Devil and Yosemite Sam, all mixed in one—and Ty Cobb. It's what he is. He's a nasty, mean, little guy who's a great teammate. He knows how to play the game, and he's clutch."

The clubhouse was fitted with all sorts of personalities, from smart-mouthed shortstop Bobby Haney to the quirky Roth to the steady Bradley to the even steadier Brown. But that locker room needed an Adrian Morales.

"We couldn't have won without Adrian Morales's leadership," Calvi said.

Chapter 10
SLUMBERING BATS

MAY 5, 2010

Every baseball season, from tee ball to the Major Leagues, has its lulls. The game's gods take as much as they give.

Enjoying a lot of success by early May, South Carolina braced for the inevitability of market correction. It just hoped the fall would not be too steep. The Gamecocks already had one swoon, in the early season series losses to East Carolina and Clemson, but they rebounded to tear through the SEC season. Spurred by the thirteen-game win streak that went into the second week of the conference schedule, South Carolina won its first seven SEC series, sweeping two of them.

The Gamecocks were 35-9 on May 5 after hitting a Carolina Stadium record seven home runs against Winthrop, including back-to-back shots by the team's first two batters, Whit Merrifield and Jackie Bradley Jr. Just when the offense seemed as if it were in a groove, it maddeningly faltered on the road at middling Kentucky, and the Gamecocks finally dropped their first SEC series. They had just four runs and ten hits in the final two games of the series, making some wonder if South Carolina was about to go south. Even the red-hot Bradley was 0 for 7 in those games.

Was this the lull?

The Gamecocks, however, showed some resilience. They followed the Kentucky series loss with a 17–4 victory against Wofford, a 10–2 win against Charleston Southern and then the first series sweep at Arkansas in South Carolina baseball history. Baum Stadium in Fayetteville, nine hundred miles from Columbia, had historically been a house of horrors for the Gamecocks and a lot of other SEC teams—but never more than South Carolina's series there in 2008.

A two-out grand slam in the bottom of the ninth capped a 12–11 Hogs rally in the Friday night game. South Carolina did not have a pulse for the series' other two games in a weekend that was fairly typical of trips to the Ozarks. But 2010 proved different.

Cooper loaded up his slingshot and outpitched Arkansas ace Drew Smyly on Friday, going to 10-0 on the season after allowing a pair of runs on three hits in seven innings. Smyly was previously 8-0.

Dyson was even stronger Saturday, providing the only regular-season performance to rival Cooper against Ole Miss. South Carolina picked up its fortieth victory of the season as Dyson threw the second complete-game shutout of the Gamecocks' season, after the school had zero in the previous five years. Dyson gave up six hits and struck out eight, throwing 123 pitches.

South Carolina trailed 3–2 in the eighth inning on Sunday, but Merrifield delivered a two-run home run to give the Gamecocks the lead. Adrian "Geico" Morales added a solo shot in the ninth. The Arkansas sweep established the fact that the Bluegrass blues from the week before were nothing more than a fluke.

Right?

Beyond the momentum and confidence provided, the Arkansas sweep set up a three-game series against Florida that would decide the SEC's Eastern Division. Florida entered the weekend 38-12. South Carolina was 42-11. Both had matching 20-7 conference records.

The Gamecocks were at home, so they figured to have the slight edge. In Cooper and Dyson, they had two veteran starters. Florida, meanwhile, started Alex Panteliodis, a sophomore, and Hudson Randall, a freshman. Neither of those Gators starters was particularly sharp, but the Gators bullpen was just as good as South Carolina's relievers had been. Jeff Barfield was the shutdown middle-inning guy in the first game. Lights-out closer Kevin Chapman picked up saves in the first two games, going a total of 3 2/3 innings to get them.

Florida won the series and the division title. South Carolina's hitters, clutch throughout the year, did not come through when opportunities presented themselves, especially with Florida's starters on the brink of disaster. The Gamecocks twice left the bases loaded against Panteliodis. Those were haunting whiffs in what was ultimately a 3–2 loss. South Carolina had fewer scoring chances in the second game, but Florida won again, 5–2, without knocking the cover off the ball.

With the SEC Tournament ahead, the Gamecocks remained confident, presuming they would respond to the series loss the same way they had against Arkansas. The No. 2 seed from the East, they thought they were a good team that had a couple of average games.

One problem: game one in the SEC Tournament was against Ole Miss. And that meant it was against Drew Pomeranz. Instead of throwing Cooper, Ray Tanner and Mark Calvi held their ace. They hoped sophomore Nolan Belcher, who had not pitched much in the season's second half, would be able to get to Jose Mata and the versatile, deep bullpen. Belcher did, and the Gamecocks held the Rebels to three runs— three more runs than South Carolina scored. Pomeranz again silenced the Gamecocks' bats for seven innings, and closer Brett Huber pitched the other two without allowing a run.

It was the first time South Carolina had been shut out in 154 games, going back to April 2008. The following day, in an elimination game against Auburn, a seventh-inning solo home run from Brady Thomas was the only thing that prevented a second consecutive shutout. The Gamecocks and Tigers were tied 1–1 until Auburn broke through with two runs in the twelfth inning to send South Carolina home.

A team that went 21-9 in the SEC's regular season was two-and-through in the conference tourney. The Gamecocks, as a team, went 14 for 75 (.187) in those two games. There was no wondering about the lull. It had arrived, and at a terrible time. The pitching remained consistent throughout, but the offense dropped to .299 for the season after spending most of it well above .300. That .299 total was with Bradley, on fire, batting .372.

Merrifield was hitting .329, much lower than expected entering June. The school's hit-streak record holder had two hitless games in his previous five after just one in the first half of the entire season. Merrifield admitted the upcoming MLB draft was eating at him. He was trying too hard to give the scouts one last impression.

"Deep down, you have a little selfish thing pulling at you," said Merrifield, a ninth-round pick who later signed with Kansas City. "You want to do the best you can to help your stock as much as you can, and make some money, hopefully. The better you do, the more money you're going to make."

That was Merrifield's reason, maybe, but what about the rest of the Gamecocks? They had to face it. They had scored one run in twenty-one innings in the SEC Tournament. They had dropped four of their final five games before the NCAA Tournament. Bradley notwithstanding, they were slumping.

The 2010 season, promising as it had felt for weeks and even months at a time, threatened to end with the same thud the past seasons few had. Would the fans stand for a seventh consecutive year without Omaha? Would the team even make it to a Super Regional for the first time since 2007?

What could the Gamecocks do to stop the slide before it was too late?

The SEC Tournament left Tanner as upset as he was following the East Carolina series. No, more, because it was nearly June and not February. The only conversations he had on the way home were with his assistants—about which scuffling players he wanted to yank from the lineup.

"I was about as unhappy as you could be," Tanner said that week. "Honestly, I wasn't good."

The confounding, directionless feeling after East Carolina led to Tanner's most identifiable tirade of the season. He didn't handle the post–SEC tourney low the same way, though. Tanner knew by then he had a good team. He faced the chore of getting it to play like one again, with the NCAA Tournament on the horizon and coming up quickly. The Gamecocks were bounced from Birmingham on a Thursday, and they would begin NCAA Regional play at home on the following Friday. That gave Tanner a week to resuscitate his team, and particularly its offense. It would practice and practice a lot, out of character for Tanner.

"We went at it," he said.

Saying Tanner went back to the basics with the Gamecocks would be an understatement.

"We were almost getting treated like Little Leaguers," said senior catcher Kyle Enders, one of the team's two captains.

South Carolina practiced five times in three days over that weekend, concluding the mini-camp of sorts with a Sunday scrimmage. It was like fall practice all over again—except a few days before the season's most important games.

"I thought the players did a nice job," Tanner said. "I thought it was meaningful."

The Gamecocks might have been miffed about the elementary fielding and hitting drills, but the way they handled it was just as significant as the work itself. They didn't get frustrated to the point that Tanner lost them. They did not lose the bond they had with one another. The Gamecocks remained their goofy selves.

When the players were asked to go through mundane throwing drills, they spiced them up by reenacting the much-advertised, overly cheesy Tom Emanski's instructional videos, endorsed by former Major Leaguer Fred McGriff and a hat that was about seven sizes too big for the Crime Dog.

"That kind of describes the team," said senior pitcher Jay Brown, the other captain. "We were still loose and trying to keep the game fun."

South Carolina got through the practices. It made them as enjoyable as possible and moved forward, hopeful they would help the team resurface for the NCAAs.

"Obviously," Enders said, "the coaches did the right thing."

Fitting that Enders later endorsed the moves. In addition to the practices, Tanner also tried to spark the team by beginning the NCAA Tournament with a drastically new lineup. Even though he was a captain and a fifth-year player, Enders was one of the Gamecocks who started the Regional on the bench.

"Something had to be done," assistant Chad Holbrook said. "We had to do something different than what we were doing. If we were going to go down, it wasn't going to be because we kept doing the same things."

Chapter 11
GETTING CRUNK

JUNE 4, 2010

The first name on Ray Tanner's lineup card for South Carolina's NCAA opener against Bucknell was a peculiar one.

Freshman Evan Marzilli had been penciled into eight of fifty-eight South Carolina starting lineups prior to that night, including just four in SEC play. Marzilli had entered a slew of games as a pinch runner or defensive replacement, but he was not a starter. Prior to the tourney, Marzilli was best known to fans for skillfully playing the national anthem on an electric guitar before the first Florida game.

It made even less sense for Marzilli to be hitting leadoff, the slot veteran Whit Merrifield had occupied for fifty-seven of the team's fifty-eight games to that point. Marzilli was the team's only other leadoff hitter—on February 20. Consider, too, that Tanner and Chad Holbrook agree Marzilli had one of the worst fall camps they had ever seen. Holbrook recalled three hits in sixty or so at-bats.

"I'm telling you," Holbrook said, "it was bad."

Marzilli didn't play poorly when he was inserted in the lineup during the course of the season, but he also did nothing to merit more playing time. Midseason, Holbrook called Marzilli into his office for a chat.

"You're one of the first players I've ever coached that could be a first-rounder, and make a lot of money, or you could never play here and never get drafted," Holbrook told him. "You have the ability to do both."

Marzilli, a kid the Gamecocks had plucked from Rhode Island, rare territory for them, looked at Holbrook as if he were nuts.

"It's time," Holbrook said, continuing, "to start listening to what you have to do as a player and what you cannot do."

From that meeting on, Holbrook described Marzilli's work ethic as "relentless." A product of that, Marzilli received a few more shots to play, even registering a pinch-hit single in South Carolina's offensively woeful SEC Tournament. Tanner saw something in Marzilli the following week. Looking for sparks at the plate, he played his hunch with Marzilli.

Tanner was confident in the decision because of his ability to press the correct buttons most of the season. With the team lacking a pronounced power punch in the middle of the lineup, Tanner had to get creative to maximize run-producing potential. The top and bottom of the order stayed generally the same, but hitters three through six were constantly being shuffled.

Tanner said he made more lineup cards in 2010 than any other year he has coached. It was roster roulette. Tanner and his staff would agonize until the wee hours figuring out the right play for a particular game or series. Sometimes the players would show up to the park and see a lineup that did not seem to make a lot of sense. But they had to learn to trust Tanner. Heck, Tanner had to learn to trust Tanner.

"I said to the team numerous times, 'We're trying very hard as a coaching staff,'" Tanner said. "'We don't have all the answers on a daily basis. We're going to make changes. We're going to go with what we believe is the right thing for the day. And it's going to change quite a bit.'"

Logically, if Marzilli was in, that meant someone was out. Starting Marzilli in right field meant that Merrifield would move to third base—probably his fifth-best position, behind all three in the outfield and second base. Merrifield's move shifted Adrian Morales to second base. But that meant Scott Wingo, the team's lovable space cadet, was on the bench. The only offensive captain, senior catcher Kyle Enders, was out, too. Senior Brady Thomas, a better hitter, was the choice behind the plate. Tanner was going with offense over defense.

Changes? This was lunacy. This was pressing a whole bunch of the buttons at the same time and seeing what happened.

As veteran leaders, it hurt Enders and Wingo. The two Greenville-area natives had played since stepping on campus, and now they had to watch the postseason? They never vented or showed their frustration, though. They took their cues from Nick Ebert, the 2009 leader in home runs and RBIs who had been relegated to the bench after freshman Christian Walker took over at first base.

Ebert worked tirelessly in the batting cage, often the first to the stadium and the last to leave after games. He rarely complained. The senior, who had turned down the New York Yankees to return to school, believed he could help the team somewhere along the line. Enders, Wingo and the rest of the team noticed, respecting Ebert more for his attitude.

"I really think the selflessness part of our team wound up being a huge component for us," Tanner said. "Guys wanted to win. Nobody wants to sit on the bench. Nobody wants to be taken out of the game. But, in the end, winning was more important to them than anything else. I felt like they really cared for each other and pulled for each other."

Wingo actually had a lot to do with building the team's unity. Immediately following the 19–6 loss to Clemson in early March, Wingo started leading "breakdowns" before each game. The affable, free-spirited junior would herd everyone together and then tell his teammates some purely fictional story that would have them laughing so hard they would cry.

Sort of like the standard *Saturday Night Live* intro, the lead-in was always different, but the end was consistently the same. Lowering himself to the ground, Wingo would yell at the top of his lungs, "I bet you won't get crunk!"

"I will!" the team would yell back. "I will!"

After three rounds of that, he'd scream, "Big dog, bark one time!" The team barked. That went on three times, ending with a bunch of barking.

Wingo heard about the ritual from a high school friend, and he introduced it to the Gamecocks. They loved it. They eagerly awaited whatever ridiculous story Wingo was going to reveal in the pregame. He always asked to be left alone in the dugout for a few minutes before the breakdown so he could conjure up his tale. Moms were involved sometimes. Umpires. Opposing players, coaches. Nothing was off limits. The stories were R-rated, at best. Anyone under fifteen would have needed earmuffs.

So even when Wingo was out of the lineup against Bucknell, he still added value to the team. Both Wingo and Enders were parts of the rain delay séance. They were laughing hysterically when Robert Beary fashioned the Avatar Spirit Stick, wildly forcing everyone in the dugout to touch it.

Enders and Wingo wound up affecting the game more directly, too. With Thomas 0 for 3, Enders entered in the seventh, walking to lead off the inning.

Wingo, pinch hitting, loaded the bases with a bunt single. Their efforts led to an important run that cut Bucknell's lead to 5–4.

Marzilli's two-run home run in the previous inning got the Gamecocks going. Fans, like the team, were getting restless before Marzilli's homer. Some at Carolina Stadium had even started to boo. They were tongue-lashing members of a forty-plus-win team that was hosting its first Regional in three seasons. Morales, who doubled just before Marzilli's home run, emphatically clapped his hands together and screamed at the crowd upon reaching second base. He stared those fans down as he crossed home plate.

South Carolina had gotten crunk.

Thanks to the séance and the spirit stick—and contributions up and down the lineup—the Gamecocks rallied to defeat Bucknell. But that was just the first game of the Regional, against the worst team in it. Third-seeded Citadel was next. The Gamecocks had defeated the Bulldogs by a combined score of 20–5 in two regular-season meetings. (South Carolina was 15-0 in midweek games.)

But for the postseason meeting, The Citadel had something South Carolina had not seen: a six-foot, four-inch, 235-pound right-handed version of Drew Pomeranz. Asher Wojciechowski was 12-2 with a 3.25 ERA entering the biggest start of his Citadel career. The Gamecocks' hope was the fact that Wojciechowski was 4-1 with a 5.14 ERA and 1.36 WHIP (walks and hits allowed per inning) in pure road starts.

Who better to oppose Wojciechowski than Blake Cooper? Wojciechowski, the 2010 draft's forty-first overall pick, had ten strikeouts through five innings. Cooper was better than the soon-to-be-first-rounder, registering ten strikeouts in the first four innings. Cooper was cruising until an error and a base hit set up a three-run home run with two outs in the fifth, putting the Bulldogs up 4–2.

The Citadel held that two-run lead into the seventh, with Wojo still going strong. With Marzilli at the plate and two on, a Wojciechowski balk moved them up a base. It also caused the seasoned starter to lose his cool. After arguing with the home plate umpire, Marzilli drove in Bobby Haney and Wingo with a single to center field. Marzilli eventually scored on a

The University of South Carolina Baseball Team's Journey
to the 2010 NCAA Championship

Wojciechowski wild pitch that went ten feet over the catcher's head. Wojo gave up five of his seven runs in the seventh.

"You've got to credit South Carolina," Citadel coach Fred Jordan said. "They beat a very good pitcher."

A two-run shot by "Geico" Morales in the ninth sealed a 9–4 victory to give the Gamecocks two come-from-behind wins in as many days in the Regional. Morales was 6 for 9—with two home runs, two doubles and two singles—in those first two games after going into the tournament with two hits in his previous twenty at-bats.

Cooper struck out a career-high twelve batters, and the four runs he allowed in 7 1/3 innings were all unearned. With his teammates' help, he had slain another giant. There were more to come.

Senior Jay Brown started the following night against second-seeded Virginia Tech. A win, and South Carolina was through to the next round. Continuing the Regional tradition, the Gamecocks quickly fell behind after a two-run home run off Brown in the first. Brown settled, though, getting the game to Jose Mata and Michael Roth, who did not allow a run in the final 5 1/3 innings. The Hokies did not score after the first.

The Gamecocks tied the game with a run in the fourth and fifth innings, and then, just as they had in the previous two Regional games, they exploded for a late crooked-number inning. Jackie Bradley Jr.'s three-run shot the highlight, South Carolina scored six runs in the sixth and went on to defeat Virginia Tech 10–2.

A team that had recently struggled with the bats scored nine, nine and ten runs in its three Regional victories, even if each required a comeback. The offense was back. It again had the pitchers' backs.

"After the pitching staff had helped us the whole year, we were able to help," said Morales, the Regional's Most Outstanding Player. "It was a never-die attitude we had. Everyone was so relaxed and not afraid of failure. That was the main thing: no one was scared to fail."

It was the first postseason baseball at two-year-old Carolina Stadium. The Gamecocks improved to 30-6 in home games in 2010, but they would not play another one since the Florida and SEC tourney skid had caused them to narrowly miss one of the eight national seeds in the NCAA Tournament. If they were going to return to Omaha for the first time since 2004, they were going to have to beat Coastal Carolina at the beach in a best-of-three.

Chapter 12
CLOSING TIME

JUNE 12, 2010

M ark Calvi's heart and mind raced as he watched Matt Price trot in from the bullpen.

Calvi took pride in his ability to put South Carolina's pitchers in the best possible positions for success. This was the opposite. He was setting the team's redshirt freshman closer up for failure.

Coastal Carolina had the bases loaded. There were no outs in the eighth inning of the teams' first Super Regional game, with the Gamecocks hanging on to a 4–3 lead. The stadium, Myrtle Beach's BB&T Coastal Field, had a 308-foot short porch in left field—and the wind was blowing out in that direction. Coastal, hitting .326 with 107 home runs and 146 doubles as a team, had a lineup every bit as potent as those they had seen in the SEC. The Chanticleers had already won fifty-five games, more than any team in college baseball would all season.

The Coastal coach's kid, Chance Gilmore, was the batter. Gilmore had twelve home runs and fifty-four RBIs—better power numbers than anyone on South Carolina's roster at the time. Oh, and he was a left-handed hitter against Price, a right-handed pitcher.

"That's the worst thing you can do to a kid," Calvi said. "I thought, 'This is the worst possible situation you could ever be in.'"

Good thing Price saw it differently than his coach.

"He looked at it as the best thing you could ever do," Calvi said. "He looked at it as a chance to show how good he was."

Price was mostly a mystery to Calvi entering 2010. Really, only one of Price's qualities was not.

"The one thing I could count on was his nuts," Calvi said. "That kid has nuts, I'm telling you."

Maybe so, but they don't get the ball over the plate. Coming off a broken wrist that forced him to redshirt, Price had what the coaches characterized as an "awful" fall camp in 2009. Calvi had a meeting with Price, a six-foot, two-inch, balding youngster from Sumter, and told him that on a ten-man staff, he would be No. 11. He told Price if there were a trip that weekend, he would be sitting at home.

"From the second he heard that, it was all over," Calvi said. "He switched. That was the moment for him."

Price went Blake Cooper–level crazy on the workouts the rest of the year. By the time the 2010 season started, Price's fastball was up from about eighty-eight to ninety miles an hour to ninety-three to ninety-five, a big difference in college ball. With that heater, Price began to pitch more confidently. Noticing that, Calvi started experimenting with Price early in the year.

In a 4–4 game against Clemson on March 6 in Greenville, Calvi and Ray Tanner called for Price to face talented Tigers freshman Richie Shaffer with two outs in the eighth inning. Kyle Parker stood on first, representing the go-ahead—and possibly winning—run. Price struck Shaffer out. The Gamecocks scored three in the top of the ninth, and Price got his first victory of the season.

"I knew it was the start of something," Calvi said. "He showed competitiveness and poise. He showed signs of being a guy for us."

In the weeks that followed, Calvi worked with Price to give him a new strategy against left-handed hitters. His change-up was not working against them. He needed another pitch—or two—to keep them off balance. First, it was an improving curveball. Then a slider unexpectedly materialized.

"It seems pretty unbelievable," said Price, who actually suggested the slider to Calvi. "I just started messing around with it, throwing it in the 'pen one day. It worked out pretty good."

Calvi entered the season thinking that John Taylor, a side-armer, would be the team's closer. By April, it was obvious that Price was the choice.

"You couldn't foresee that coming," Calvi said. "I told the staff we needed a closer. We needed a closer or a couple of guys that could save sixteen games between them. Matt Price went out there and said, 'I'm your closer.'"

Price had eight saves and a sub-3 ERA entering the Super Regional, but he had never entered a game to find this sort of jam. South Carolina up a run in the eighth, Coastal had the bases loaded with none out. Getting out of the bind with one run in would be a realistically positive outcome, Tanner thought. Going to the bottom of the eighth in a tie game would have been a good result.

Price had set a different goal for the inning. Gilmore struck out swinging. Taylor Motter, the next batter, then struck out looking. Suddenly, with two outs, the unthinkable became a distinct possibility. With one more out, Price would escape the jam to end all jams. With one more out, Calvi would have license to again breathe.

Daniel Bowman hit the ball hard, but back to Price. He flipped over to Christian Walker at first base, fist-pumping and shouting as he strutted to the South Carolina dugout. The Gamecocks had done far more than dodge a bullet; Price had maneuvered the team around a landmine.

Coastal had the tying run on second base in the ninth against Price, but the Chants' leading hitter, Tommy La Stella (.378), flied out to end the game.

"I don't know, even now, how I did it," Price said the following week. "I just knew if I went in there and pounded the strike zone, and threw my off-speed [pitches] for strikes, that I was going to get the job done and keep our team in position."

Afterward, Coastal coach Gary Gilmore scratched his head in disbelief. He blamed scouting reports, saying they had not indicated Price threw that hard. Evidently, he had gotten a hold of some old info—bad info. He had not heard about Price version 2.0. That made Calvi laugh the following week.

"Well," he said, "that's why they couldn't hit him."

South Carolina was one win away from Omaha, but the Gamecocks knew Coastal would not give them a free pass to the College World Series. The contentious first game only increased existing tensions between the two fan bases.

The University of South Carolina Baseball Team's Journey to the 2010 NCAA Championship

About 125 miles separate the two campuses, and yet, from how often the schools have met athletically, CCU might as well stand for Coastal Connecticut or Coastal California. The Gamecocks and Chants had played just twice since Tanner and Gilmore took over their respective programs in the late 1990s, even though a handful of in-state opponents are always a part of both teams' schedules.

The hiatus, which carried into other sports, such as football, was not coincidental. Coastal spent thirty years within the University of South Carolina's system before breaking off and becoming independent in 1993. The decision strained relationships among the schools' leaders.

So when Coastal was named the NCAA Tournament's No. 4 overall seed in 2010, with South Carolina placed in its portion of the bracket, the Chants knew they had a chance to make a good deal of history. A program on the rise under Gilmore, certainly, Coastal had never been to the College World Series. What better way to get there than to take out South Carolina?

At 55-8, this was the Chants' best chance. They had gone 25-0 in Big South play. They had about a half-dozen pro prospects. They had 271 extra-base hits. The top two hitters in the lineup had 110 stolen bases in 130 tries. They had a couple of front-line starting pitchers they believed could have excelled anywhere.

And as opposed to the program's only other Super Regional appearance in 2008, when North Carolina routed Coastal, this time the Chants were at home. Sensing Gamecocks fans could take over the ballpark the same way Clemson had in the 2007 Regional, which the Tigers won, Coastal fans snapped up as many tickets as possible, beginning literally minutes after the Regional-clinching win against the College of Charleston on that Monday.

Some fans bought as many as ninety seats for each Super Regional game. They preferred to sell them to friends or give them away—heck, burn the tickets—rather than see garnet in the stands. As a result, the entire three-game series was sold out by Tuesday morning, hours before tickets were to go on sale online. South Carolina fans, zealous and large in number, were not happy.

Fans aside, Gilmore knew his team would still have to find a way to beat the Gamecocks twice.

"South Carolina, they've done it all," Gilmore said. "The opportunity in front of Coastal Carolina, it doesn't just change our team. It changes our school, our community. Two more wins, and it'll be the most insane thing this school has ever gone through."

South Carolina had been to Omaha eight times, but not since 2004. The current players had never been. It was the last chance for the seniors and drafted juniors such as Whit Merrifield.

"You can taste it. You really can," Merrifield said just before the series. "We're two huge wins away. Two wins seem like such a small task, but that's such a big, big thing to accomplish. We know we're so close. We're hungry for it. I don't think any team in the country wants it as bad as we do."

Price and the pitching proved that in game one. When Dyson stumbled in the second game, it was up to Merrifield and the team's hitters.

Chapter 13
POWERING ON

JUNE 13, 2010

South Carolina trailed Coastal Carolina by two runs with two outs in the eighth inning when Ray Tanner climbed the dugout stairs. With Jackie Bradley Jr. standing at the plate, Tanner whistled to call the next two hitters, Adrian Morales and Christian Walker, over to him.

"Jackie's going to get on," Tanner told the pair of 2010 newcomers. "Walker can't hit a home run, Adrian, unless you get on base."

It was a hopeful forecast from Tanner considering that Whit Merrifield had just grounded into a momentum-killing double play. Also, entering that second Super Regional game, the Chanticleers were 48-0 when leading after seven innings.

Tanner's comedic timing was strong, though. By mentioning the optimal results, addressing that elephant in the huddle with them, Tanner had comforted Morales and Walker.

He also proved prophetic.

South Carolina might have transitioned to become more of a scratch-out-runs, smallball sort of team, but that didn't mean Tanner wanted to abandon the home run altogether. There is no quicker way to extend leads or erase deficits. There is no better way to pack a park. Would more Gamecocks fans rather see a sacrifice bunt—or a five-hundred-foot blast that sails over the right-field wall and hits a warehouse across Williams Street?

Tanner recruited Walker to hit home runs. It had not worked out that way, though, in his freshman year. Walker had six home runs in 172 at-bats entering the Super Regional. Plucky second baseman Scott Wingo, known for his defense, had nine.

What gave? The track record was there. As a high school senior, Walker was invited to the International Power Showcase in St. Petersburg, Florida. He won the home run derby, smacking nineteen homers to beat Bryce Harper—the No. 1 overall pick in the 2010 MLB draft.

Walker arrived at South Carolina with the same prowess. He was the opposite of Evan Marzilli, putting together one of the best fall camps the coaching staff had ever seen.

"No one was as good as he was. No one," Tanner said. "And I'm talking about some of the guys who are in the big leagues right now. I've just never had a hitter be that consistent. He could spray the ball all over the field. It just came naturally for him."

Tanner assumed that Walker would start opening day—and stay in the lineup until he was drafted three years later.

With the 2009 home run leader, Nick Ebert, at first and Walker at third, Tanner felt sure the Gamecocks would get plenty of power from their corner infielders. And the season started promisingly enough for Walker. The Philadelphia-area native homered in his first game. He homered and drove in five runs the following day. Tanner had hit the jackpot with Walker. Why wasn't this kid in spring training somewhere?

The answer would come soon enough. Walker hit four home runs the rest of the regular season, just two in SEC play. His batting average tumbled to .239 by April 14. Walker's playing time dwindled along with his average. Behind closed doors, Tanner chided Walker for reading too many headlines about himself. Tanner asserted that it had led to overconfidence.

"I was tough on him," Tanner said. "I was probably too hard on him."

Tanner later blamed himself for Walker's struggles. He said he praised Walker too much, too soon. Tough-love moments included, Walker said the coaches and players stuck by him. He thought he would get another shot. He didn't know when, but he believed it would come.

A grand slam as the designated hitter against Ole Miss on April 17 awoke the offensive star in him. Walker did most of his damage, though, by keeping the ball in the ballpark. He hit .511 (23 for 45) in his next thirteen games to vault his average to .328, an extremely difficult thing to do in the heart of the conference season. Walker wound up leading the team with a .346 average against SEC teams. Tanner marveled that the freshman did not get too down on himself. The six-foot, 210-pound hulk had shown he was just as tough mentally as physically.

"Once I got my mindset back to where I thought it should be," Walker said, "everything started coming back around for me."

With the games gaining importance, Walker was emerging as one of the players Tanner most wanted at the plate. To that point, game two of the Myrtle Beach Super Regional was South Carolina's most important game of the season. And Walker was at the plate in a big spot.

Just as Tanner said, Bradley got on base. Tiring Coastal closer Austin Fleet walked him. That brought up Morales. The Gamecocks didn't need insurance. Trailing 9–7 and down to their final four outs, they needed Geico to be a hero. Morales admitted after the game that he had one thing on his mind: game-tying home run. Morales swung for the fence. He just missed, but a double moved Bradley to third and put Morales, who represented the tying run, on second.

Walker came to the plate with Tanner's prophecy still going to form.

Fleet struck Walker out looking in the sixth inning, with a slider on the outside corner. Fleet started him off in the eighth with the same pitch. Walker took it for a strike. The second pitch was an effort to copy the first. It was a hair farther outside, but umpire David Rogers still called it a strike. Just like that, Walker was in a 0-2 hole. Trying to get Walker to chase, Fleet put a slider in the dirt. Walker was still behind.

Given the recent trend, Walker, 3 for 9 so far in the Super, was of course expecting a slider. He got one. But Fleet, in since the sixth inning, misfired. The pitch caught way too much of the plate, and Walker belted it. It was a no-doubter. The ball sailed well over the short fence in left field for a three-run home run. It almost left BB&T Coastal Field completely.

Walker flipped his bat to the screen and ran, screaming, to first base with his arms extended down to his sides. He smacked hands with first base coach Sammy Esposito and embarked on a 270-foot journey he will never forget. "That was definitely one of the better jogs I've taken in my life," he said.

Bradley and Morales trotted across the plate to tie the game and then they waited, along with the rest of the team, for Walker. The Avatar Spirit Stick was there, too. Walker touched home to make it 10–9, Gamecocks.

"I hit it and, before I knew it, I was touching home plate and everybody was smacking me on the head," Walker said. "I've tried to describe it and explain it to people, but it's impossible. Being there, it was unreal." In a single swing, Walker had realized his prodigious reputation.

"He's a special player," Tanner said after the game. "He certainly couldn't have come up any bigger than he did today."

Closer Matt Price was gassed from the previous day, but Betty White could have gotten the Chants out after Walker's homer. They were done. Price pitched a 1-2-3 ninth to close out a victory that put the Gamecocks back in the College World Series for the first time in six seasons.

"Really, I'm at a loss for words," Tanner said afterward. "We found a way. We were just one run better two days in a row."

One sobering thought did counter the rush of the College World Series berth. Before the Super Regional, assistant Chad Holbrook learned that Bayler Teal would not receive any additional treatment for the disease he had battled since September 2008. As much as it hurt, the Teals had conceded to cancer.

Following his stay earlier in the year at Sloan-Kettering in New York, Bayler received some radiation and light chemotherapy treatments in Columbia. It was pointless, though. Bayler's body rejected every form of medication. The family knew then it was a matter of when for Bayler, and not if. Each day would be treated like a treasure.

Before heading to Coastal, Holbrook again told the Teals that the Gamecocks would play for Bayler. They won two dramatic Super Regional games with him in mind. Those victories were more soothing to Bayler than any medicine the world could offer. Holbrook called Bayler's dad, Rob, just after Walker's home run.

Holbrook told Teal the Gamecocks intended to win the College World Series for Bayler.

Chapter 14
WEATHERING STORMS

JUNE 20, 2010

An *Avatar* sequel is on the way. South Carolina's baseball team didn't bother to wait before creating its own version.

The initial séance during a weather delay spurred the offense to score eight unanswered runs in a victory against Bucknell to begin the NCAA Tournament. The Gamecocks had not lost since, winning five consecutive games to reach Omaha for the first time in six years.

Go figure that rain was in the forecast for South Carolina's College World Series opener against Oklahoma. A four-and-a-half-hour delay before the first pitch turned an early afternoon start at Rosenblatt Stadium into a night game. The teams got through five and a half innings before lightning again halted play.

The Gamecocks were not playing terribly. They trailed 3–2 and had home runs from Super Regional hero Christian Walker and unofficial team MVP Jackie Bradley Jr. But something called out to the team. It was time to return to "Pandora."

Chanting and swaying in the dark had worked once. Why not again?

Forget a séance; the Gamecocks should have been in the locker room celebrating the fact that they had scored.

Walker's second-inning home run marked the first time a South Carolina team had put a run on the board in its College World Series opener since 1982. Ronald Reagan was in office. Survivor's "Eye of the Tiger" dominated the music charts. The current players were not even close to being born.

The Gamecocks had been shut out in their past four Omaha openers, outscored 22–0 in those games. That included all three with Ray Tanner as coach, from 2002 to 2004. All told, South Carolina had lost its previous six openers, with the only wins in the program's eight prior appearances coming in 1975 and 1977.

Losing the opener in the double-elimination event makes it all but impossible to win the tournament—to win the national title. It's playing without a safety net for the entire stay. The pressure eventually tightens enough that the team is soon on a plane destined for home. It's too much to overcome, relative to the talent in the eight-team field. A College World Series champ had not lost its first game since Southern Cal in 1998.

To South Carolina's credit, despite the issues in the opener, it still held a 16-17 overall record in the College World Series going into 2010. The Gamecocks had played well with no room for error, even if it was not the ideal position. The prime example of that was 2002, when South Carolina defeated rival Clemson—routing the Tigers, 12–4 and 10–2—in elimination games to reach the national title game against Texas. Fatigued, the Gamecocks had little left for the Longhorns in the final, falling 12–6. Unfortunately for South Carolina, that was the last tournament before organizers implemented a best-of-three national championship series in 2003.

The goal against Oklahoma, obviously, was to avoid a seventh consecutive loss in an opener. Surely, the séance would be what was missing, to exorcise thirty-three years of College World Series demons.

Starting pitcher Blake Cooper had to come out after the second delay, which lasted two hours and pushed the game deep into the Nebraska night. Cooper had thrown just sixty-seven pitches, but the layoff was too long from which to return. He had been atypically off all night, often missing his spots. Cooper gave up three runs on six hits in five innings.

It was a wonder Cooper started at all. After exiting game one of the Super Regional, he was hit in the dugout by a line drive. Of all places, the ball somehow struck his pitching hand. An X-ray exam showed there were no breaks, but Cooper's right hand was bruised, swollen and sore. There was nothing short of a fracture, though, that would have prevented Cooper from his first College World Series start. Even then, he would have begged to pitch.

The University of South Carolina Baseball Team's Journey to the 2010 NCAA Championship

"Battling" was a word Tanner and the Gamecocks used in Omaha as much as "the," and Cooper had battled against the Sooners. With far from his best stuff, the team was down a run, very much in the game.

Still 3–2 in the seventh, South Carolina had the tying run on second base with one out. Brady Thomas stayed there, though, after shortstop Bobby Haney and pinch hitter Nick Ebert struck out to end the threat against Sooners reliever Jeremy Erben. Erben was tiring in the eighth when he loaded the bases by consecutively walking Adrian Morales and Walker with two outs. Thomas swung at the first pitch. He hit it hard, but to the right fielder. Oklahoma again avoided trouble.

When runs are at a premium in such a big game, missing scoring opportunities such as those becomes weighty to a team. The psychological burden became even greater when Oklahoma's Garrett Buechele homered off Jose Mata in the eighth. Down 4–2, if the Gamecocks were to rally, they would have to do it in the ninth against Sooners closer Ryan Duke.

Kyle Enders and pinch hitter Robert Beary, the spirit stick's creator, led off with back-to-back singles. Adam Matthews, though, was overpowered. He struck out, failing to even move the runners. Leadoff hitter Evan Marzilli drew a walk to load the bases with one out and Whit Merrifield coming up. But Merrifield popped harmlessly into foul ground beyond third base.

With two down, hope was not yet gone. South Carolina still had Bradley at the plate with the bases loaded in a two-run game. Oklahoma showed a great deal of respect to the sophomore, pitching around him to walk in a run. It was 4–3, with Morales coming up. Beary represented the tying run at third base. Marzilli, at second, was the go-ahead run.

Even though Duke had walked two of the past three batters, Morales swung at the first pitch. The fly ball to center field ended the game. From the seventh inning on, the Gamecocks were 0 for 7 with runners in scoring position, twice letting tiring relievers off the hook by swinging at the first pitch. Oklahoma held on, and South Carolina fell to the College World Series losers' bracket for the seventh consecutive time.

Maybe the second séance worked on a delay?

The game deserved an asterisk. The Gamecocks and Sooners arrived at the park before noon and left Rosenblatt Stadium just before midnight. The two separate weather delays, more than six hours in length, meant the game took eight hours and ten minutes to play. Good luck settling into a rhythm.

"That was not an easy day for either team," said Sunny Golloway, Oklahoma's ironically named coach. "I kept looking at my watch."

The final couple of innings were played with lightning streaking across and illuminating the sky. Some thought the game should have been stopped again, but the lightning did not set off the stadium's sensors. Good thing. Another delay would have pushed the game's conclusion to Monday. Sunday's other game, Arizona State and Clemson, was already moved back a day.

The feeling Sunday night, and into Monday, was that top-seeded Arizona State would crush Clemson and set up an elimination game Tuesday between the Palmetto State's top programs.

The Tigers did not share that sentiment. Clemson instead played like the nation's No. 1 team, taking out Arizona State on Monday morning, 6–3. The Sun Devils were 51-8 entering the College World Series, one of three national seeds remaining in the field—and the only one on their side of the bracket. The buzz in Omaha was that this was their event to lose. Arizona State had already won five national championships. But a game that started at 9:18 a.m. Mountain time ended with the Sun Devils in the losers' bracket with the Gamecocks.

Arizona State was even punchier Tuesday. A lineup that hit .338 in the regular season, the best among the teams in Omaha, was in a coma against the Gamecocks. The pitching was even more out of it. Starter Merrill Kelly was 10-2 with a 3.57 ERA coming in. But Kelly did not make it out of the second inning, giving up eight runs on ten hits in 1 2/3 innings.

South Carolina led 8–0 through two innings and 10–0 through three. Sam Dyson went 7 1/3 innings, and the Gamecocks breezed to an 11–4 victory. The odds-on favorite to win the College World Series was headed home. The Sun Devils never showed, really.

It was the first time since the NCAA Tournament expanded to sixty-four teams, in 1999, that a No. 1 overall seed had gone 0-for-Omaha. The eight previous No. 1 seeds that reached the College World Series had won at least one game. Coming in, Arizona State had not lost consecutive games all season. Two teams from the same small state, Clemson and South Carolina, made that a reality. Their side of the bracket was now wide open. An unseeded team was guaranteed to play for the national title. If it was not Oklahoma, it would be a team from the Palmetto State.

Clemson, in its twelfth College World Series, then moved a step closer to its first national championship by defeating Oklahoma in the winners' bracket. That meant two things for the Gamecocks: if they wanted to continue playing, they would have to beat the team that had handed them their only NCAA Tournament loss. And if they wanted to play for, and win, a national title, they would have to defeat Clemson twice—just like in 2002.

OKLAHOMA
JUNE 20, 2010, ROSENBLATT STADIUM, OMAHA, NEBRASKA

OKLAHOMA 4 (50-16)

Player	ab	r	h	rbi	bb	so	po	a	lob
Chris Ellison cf	3	1	1	0	1	0	2	0	0
Max White lf	3	0	0	0	0	2	3	0	0
Garrett Buechele 3b	4	1	1	1	0	1	2	0	0
Tyler Ogle c	4	0	1	1	0	0	5	2	1
Cody Reiner rf	4	1	2	0	0	0	1	0	0
Kaleb Herren rf	0	0	0	0	0	0	0	0	0
Cameron Seitzer 1b	2	0	0	0	0	2	6	2	2
Danny Black 2b	3	0	0	0	0	2	4	3	0
Caleb Bushyhead ss	3	1	2	2	0	0	1	2	1
Eric Ross dh	2	0	0	0	0	0	0	0	1
Ricky Eisenberg ph	1	0	0	0	0	0	0	0	0
Michael Rocha p	0	0	0	0	0	2	0	0	0
Jeremy Erben p	0	0	0	0	0	0	1	1	0
Ryan Duke p	0	0	0	0	0	0	0	0	0
Totals	29	4	7	4	1	9	25	10	5

SOUTH CAROLINA 3 (48-16)

Player	ab	r	h	rbi	bb	so	po	a	lob
Evan Marzilli lf	3	0	0	0	2	0	4	0	0
Whit Merrifield rf/3b	4	0	1	0	1	0	0	0	0
Jackie Bradley Jr. cf	4	1	2	2	1	1	2	0	0
Adrian Morales 3b/2b	4	0	0	0	1	1	2	3	4
Christian Walker 1b	3	1	2	1	1	0	7	0	0
Brady Thomas dh	4	0	2	0	0	0	0	0	3
Kyle Enders c	2	1	1	0	1	0	7	0	0
Bobby Haney ss	3	0	0	0	0	1	1	1	2
Robert Beary ph	1	0	1	0	0	0	0	0	0
Scott Wingo 2b	2	0	0	0	0	0	1	0	0
Nick Ebert ph	1	0	0	0	0	1	0	0	1
Adam Matthews rf	1	0	0	0	0	1	0	0	0
Blake Cooper p	0	0	0	0	0	0	0	2	0
Michael Roth p	0	0	0	0	0	0	0	0	0
John Taylor p	0	0	0	0	0	0	0	0	0
Steven Neff p	0	0	0	0	0	0	0	0	0
Jose Mata p	0	0	0	0	0	0	0	0	0
Tyler Webb p	0	0	0	0	0	0	0	0	0
Totals	**32**	**3**	**9**	**3**	**7**	**5**	**24**	**6**	**10**

Score by Innings				R H E
South Carolina	010	100	001	- 3 9 0
Oklahoma	110	100	01X	- 4 7 0

DP—OU 1. LOB—SC 10; OU 5. HR—Bradley (12); Walker (8); Buechele (17); Bushyhead (6). HBP—Seitzer. SH—Enders (5); White (4); Seitzer (5). SB—Ellison (24). CS—Thomas (2).

The University of South Carolina Baseball Team's Journey to the 2010 NCAA Championship

South Carolina	ip	h	r	er	bb	so	ab	bf	np
Blake Cooper	5.0	6	3	3	1	5	19	22	67
Michael Roth	1.0	0	0	0	0	1	3	4	19
John Taylor	0.1	0	0	0	0	0	1	1	2
Steven Neff	0.1	0	0	0	0	0	1	1	1
Jose Mata	0.2	1	1	1	0	0	3	3	12
Tyler Webb	0.2	0	0	0	0	1	2	2	12

Oklahoma	ip	h	r	er	bb	so	ab	bf	np
Michael Rocha	6.0	5	2	2	3	2	20	23	86
Jeremy Erben	2.0	4	1	1	2	2	9	12	55
Ryan Duke	1.0	0	0	0	2	1	3	5	19

Win—Rocha (8-2). Loss—Cooper (12-2). Save—None.
HBP—by Roth (Seitzer). Erben faced 2 batters in the 9th.

Umpires—HP: Kelly Gonzalez; 1B: Gus Rodriguez; 2B: David Savage; 3B: Mark Ditsworth
Start: 6:25 p.m. Time: 2:53 Attendance: 22,835

Game notes
Start of game delayed 4:15 by rain.
Game delayed for 2:01 prior to bottom of 6th inning.

Arizona State
June 22, 2004, Rosenblatt Stadium, Omaha, Nebraska

South Carolina 11 (49-16)

Player	ab	r	h	rbi	bb	so	po	a	lob
Evan Marzilli lf	4	2	2	0	0	1	4	0	0
Whit Merrifield rf	5	2	3	2	0	0	3	0	0
Jackie Bradley Jr. cf	4	1	3	4	0	0	0	0	0
Christian Walker 1b	4	0	0	1	1	1	7	1	1
Brady Thomas dh	3	1	1	0	0	1	0	0	2
Adam Matthews ph/dh	2	0	0	0	0	1	0	0	0
Adrian Morales 3b	5	2	2	2	0	1	0	2	4
Kyle Enders c	4	1	1	0	0	2	7	0	0
Bobby Haney ss	4	0	1	0	0	1	4	3	0
Scott Wingo 2b	3	2	1	2	1	1	1	5	0
Sam Dyson p	0	0	0	0	0	0	1	0	0
Matt Price p	0	0	0	0	0	0	0	0	0
Totals	**38**	**11**	**14**	**11**	**2**	**9**	**27**	**11**	**7**

Arizona State 4 (52-10)

Player	ab	r	h	rbi	bb	so	po	a	lob
Drew Maggi ss	5	0	1	1	0	1	2	2	3
Zack MacPhee 2b	5	0	1	0	0	0	0	2	1
Kole Calhoun rf	4	1	1	0	1	1	0	0	2
Riccio Torrez 1b	3	0	0	0	0	2	10	1	0
Johnny Ruettiger lf/cf	5	1	2	0	0	2	1	0	2
Deven Marrero dh	4	1	3	1	0	0	0	0	0
Drew Aplin cf	2	1	0	0	1	0	2	0	2
Matt Newman ph/lf	1	0	1	1	0	0	0	0	0
Raoul Torrez 3b	3	0	0	0	0	0	0	4	0
Austin Barnes c	4	0	2	1	0	1	9	1	0
Merrill Kelly p	0	0	0	0	0	0	0	0	0
Mitchell Lambson p	0	0	0	0	0	0	0	0	0
Jordan Swagerty p	0	0	0	0	0	0	0	0	0
Totals	**36**	**4**	**11**	**4**	**2**	**7**	**24**	**10**	**10**

The University of South Carolina Baseball Team's Journey to the 2010 NCAA Championship

Score by Innings				R H E
Arizona State	000	020	020	- 4 11 0
South Carolina	082	000	01X	- 11 14 0

DP—SC 2. LOB—ASU 10; SC 7. 2B—Marrero (12); Haney (7); Wingo (8). HR—Merrifield (13); Bradley (13); Morales (9). HBP—Torrez, Ri. 2; Torrez, Ra.; Marzilli; Bradley. SB—Maggi (36); MacPhee (20).

Arizona State	ip	h	r	er	bb	so	ab	bf	np
Merrill Kelly	1.2	10	8	8	0	3	15	15	48
Mitchell Lambson	4.1	2	2	2	2	4	15	19	70
Jordan Swagerty	2.0	2	1	1	0	2	8	8	28

South Carolina	ip	h	r	er	bb	so	ab	bf	np
Sam Dyson	7.1	8	4	4	2	3	28	32	120
Matt Price	1.2	3	0	0	0	4	8	9	38

Win—Dyson (6-5). Loss—Kelly (10-3). Save—None.

HBP—by Dyson (Torrez, Ri.); by Lambson (Marzilli); by Lambson (Bradley); by Dyson (Torrez, Ri.); by Price (Torrez, Ra.).

Umpires—HP: David Savage; 1B: Mark Ditsworth; 2B: Kelly Gonzales; 3B: Gus Rodriguez
Start: 3:35 p.m.   Time: 3:09   Attendance: 19,936

Game notes
Elimination game for both teams.

Chapter 15
LOOKING UP

JUNE 24, 2010

E ver since South Carolina's baseball team stepped into a hospital room in October 2008 to find a cancer-stricken boy laughing and bouncing on a couch, Bayler Teal had taught the Gamecocks about survival.

So it was a strange word to use as they played in the College World Series. The word had been redefined by Bayler. Talking about surviving in a baseball tournament, compared to a seven-year-old life, felt hollow.

Athletic teams visit sick kids all the time, but Bayler was not a community service endeavor. He had become a friend to the Gamecocks. He had become one of them. They played for him at Georgia, sweeping the Bulldogs. They played for him again in the Super Regional, knocking out Coastal Carolina in dramatic fashion to advance to the school's first College World Series since 2004.

Just before the team left for Omaha, assistant coach Chad Holbrook went on the Gamecocks' flagship radio station in Columbia and told fans the team would again play for Bayler. Holbrook made sure Bayler was listening when he made the announcement. Bayler was weak, but he managed a smile. He still could not believe the team was playing for him.

It had been about a week since doctors at Palmetto Health Children's Hospital determined that treating Bayler was useless. With the decision to stop the chemo and radiation, his parents had been robbed of the hope they had pinned everything to for nearly two years. It was a crushing letdown that would end with the loss of their son. Only one question remained: how much time did they have left with him?

Rob was distraught on the Wednesday following South Carolina's College World Series win against Arizona State. He said he thought Bayler had a few months to live, but the idea of his son in pain tortured him. Rob had been so positive and upbeat throughout. But all optimism was gone. By then, he had been defeated by cancer just as much as Bayler.

"We kind of knew it was over," he said later.

Bayler had a scan the previous week, and the cancer, doctors told the Teals, was "everywhere."

The week South Carolina went to the College World Series was also the week Bayler received the best gift of his life. Worn down by the illness, Bayler still found the energy to drive his new Gamecock-themed golf cart all over the neighborhood. He loved it.

Bayler was in it during the late afternoon hours on that Wednesday when he pulled over in the front yard. He complained to his mom and dad that he wanted to go to the hospital. The only reason he usually wanted to go there was to play games and mess with his favorite doctors and nurses. This was different. Bayler had a way of masking his pain, but he could not hide it any longer.

His dad said he knew it was the last trip to the hospital. But how long would he have to watch the injustice of his son's suffering? The question pierced his heart.

"I'm ready for him to be out of this," Rob said, his voice unsteady. "This is unfair."

The Teals had waged war against cancer, against the monster, for twenty-two months. They surrendered that Thursday. At 9:00 a.m., Bayler was given a strong dosage of morphine to help with the pain. At 10:00 a.m., as he drifted in and out of consciousness, he offered his last words. His parents were adjusting his pillow, and he asked if they could do it later.

The day became more difficult for the Teals as it progressed. All afternoon, Rob and Risha talked with Bayler's little brother, five-year-old Bridges. They told him he needed to say goodbye to his brother. They told him it was the last time he would see his best friend.

The Teals felt all day the warmth from friends and family who had been with them every step of the way. Bayler always had a wealth of support, and a lot of it was present at the hospital. The outpouring was a blessing, but it also made it difficult for Rob and Risha to spend any time alone with Bayler. Someone was always in the room with them.

The traffic slowly dissipated into the evening hours until, around 8:00 p.m., Rob's aunt was kneeling in prayer at the end of the bed. Seeing Bayler in pain, she prayed for God to take him. She prayed for Bayler's ultimate healing. She said amen and stood, hugging two exhausted parents as she left the room around 9:00 p.m.

Rob and Risha were finally alone with their sleeping son. Sticking with their hospital tradition, Risha changed into pajamas and crawled into bed with Bayler, snuggling beside him. Rob squeezed his son's hand. Not sure what else to do, he turned on the room's television to see how the Gamecocks were faring against Oklahoma.

All was calm. His parents were with him. His Gamecocks were on TV. Five minutes later, Bayler's breathing changed.

"I believe he waited for that," Rob said, "and he let go."

In a hospital bed in Columbia, Bayler took his final breath at 9:32 p.m. On a baseball field in Omaha, the Gamecocks tied their College World Series game against Oklahoma at 9:32 p.m.

It was as if energy transferred instantaneously from Bayler to his team. The timing of the events, down to the minute, was incredibly difficult to explain. Still is.

South Carolina had not scored against Oklahoma in 7 1/3 innings until Christian Walker's RBI single got through the left side of the Sooners infield. Walker had come through at Coastal Carolina with the Gamecocks down to their final four outs, but this was with five outs remaining in their season. They were 0 for 6 with runners in scoring position at that point.

Things played out a lot differently for South Carolina after 9:32 p.m.

Back in Columbia, Rob and Risha were unsure what to do. They were numb. It was as if they had run the length of a marathon only to find no finish line. They had fought so long that they had no idea how to suddenly lay down their arms. So they fell into their family's arms.

Leaving the hospital, Rob picked up Bayler's pillow. It had a Gamecock on it. That caused Rob to turn his head toward the TV. He saw that South Carolina had tied the game. That sparked Rob to pass along the bad news to Holbrook.

The University of South Carolina Baseball Team's Journey to the 2010 NCAA Championship

For some reason he still cannot identify, Holbrook thought to check his phone in the dugout. In the ninth inning, he picked it up to see a text message from Rob: "Bayler is in Heaven."

Holbrook knew Bayler was back in the hospital, but the message still shocked his system. Even in the late innings of a game that could end his team's season, Holbrook was floored. He decided he would not tell the team about Bayler until afterward. He didn't want to introduce new emotions in an already intense environment. But with what he had learned, Holbrook was a wreck in the third-base coaching box.

"I remember looking up to the sky and saying, 'We need you here, big man,'" Holbrook said.

Asking out loud for help from above was something Holbrook had done throughout his coaching career. Including his mother, who succumbed to cancer, he had lost several friends and loved ones over the years. Holbrook didn't know if they could help him and his teams from beyond the grave, but he wanted to believe they could. That was enough to comfort and calm him, even in the tensest times on the diamond. In fact, he had asked for divine aid from this same Rosenblatt coaching box. In 2006 and 2007, North Carolina advanced to the national championship series. The Tar Heels lost both times. With a new school and Bayler watching, maybe this time would be different.

The game went into extra innings, still tied 1–1. Oklahoma catcher Tyler Ogle broke the deadlock with a solo home run off Ethan Carter in the twelfth inning. How would the Gamecocks escape from this one?

Robert Beary, creator of the Avatar Spirit Stick, led off the bottom of the inning with a single. Marzilli struck out, failing to move Beary into scoring position. But Beary did that on his own, stealing second.

Whit Merrifield then popped to third for the second out, leaving Beary on second base. That brought up the team's best hitter, Bradley, with South Carolina down to its final out of the season.

In the first game against Oklahoma and the win against Arizona State, Bradley was 5 for 8 with two home runs and six RBIs. He was hitting .400 in the NCAA Tournament and riding an eighteen-game hit streak that started in mid-May. But going into that twelfth-inning at-bat, Bradley was 0 for 5; he had hit only one ball out of the infield all night.

Sooners closer Ryan Duke started Bradley with a fastball on the outer half of the plate, and Bradley took it for a called strike. Duke then missed with the next two pitches, putting Bradley in a 2-1 count, a hitter's count. Bradley took a big hack at the next pitch, a fastball up, and fouled it off down the left-field line.

The Gamecocks were down to their final strike of the year.

Holbrook's two boys, Reece and Cooper, were crying in the stands. They did not want to go home. The expressions worn by South Carolina's adult fans were not much more positive. They did not want to go home, either. One more out, though, and it was over. One more strike, and it was over.

Duke's 2-2 pitch was inside—but it was close.

"I even heard the pitcher kind of yell out a little bit. Like, 'Yeah!'" Bradley said. "Like he knew that he'd struck me out. And I was thinking, 'No, that wasn't a strike.'"

Home plate umpire A.J. Lostaglio, whose opinion mattered most, agreed. Everyone took a deep breath and prepared for the 3-2 pitch. The Gamecocks were doing their "whiskey" routine over the dugout rail, cupping and wiggling their hands. Patrick Sullivan had the Avatar Spirit Stick under his nose, with his lips pressed against it.

Duke grimaced as soon as he let go of the 3-2 offering. His fastball caught too much of the plate, and Bradley roped the ball under the first baseman's glove and into right field. Beary roared around third base and touched home. The game was tied, 2–2.

Shaken, Duke walked the next batter, reserve infielder Jeff Jones, on four pitches. Representing the game-winning run, Bradley moved to second base. That brought up designated hitter Brady Thomas. Like Bradley prior to his at-bat, the team's backup catcher was 0 for 5 on the night.

Thomas's time at the plate did not last long. The senior who did not even have an at-bat in the Super Regional hit a ninety-one-mile-an-hour fastball off the bottom of his bat. It glanced off the front of the mound and skipped into center field. The Sooners outfielder did not even try to make a play.

The Gamecocks had won.

For style points, Bradley slid into home plate. Adrian Morales welcomed him with open arms, bear-hugging Bradley after he popped up from the dirt. The team mobbed Bradley—and then sprinted across the infield to pounce on Thomas.

Good thing Oklahoma didn't realize what Holbrook did: Bradley missed third base on his way home. If the Sooners appealed, the game would have continued into the thirteenth. Who knows what would have happened then? Bradley denied missing the bag when Holbrook confronted him about it after the game. In the fall, though, Bradley sheepishly admitted that Holbrook was right.

They could at least laugh about it by then.

A Gamecocks supporter from birth, Bayler Teal, six months old, sports a replica jersey of one of his dad's favorite football players, Ryan Brewer. Teal was born December 24, 2002, in Florence. *Courtesy of the Teal family.*

Above, left: In September 2008, eleven days before being diagnosed with cancer, Bayler Teal dresses up as a Gamecocks football player. *Courtesy of the Teal family.*

Above, right: Bayler Teal, age seven, prepares to show his power stroke on the Little League field. Despite the effects from cancer, Teal managed the strength to play a season of baseball with his brother, Bridges. *Courtesy of the Teal family.*

Coach Ray Tanner, *far right*, watches as former Gamecocks coaches June Raines and Bobby Richardson cut a ribbon to open Carolina Stadium in February 2009. *Courtesy of Juan Blas/TheBigSpur.com.*

Third baseman Adrian Morales dances off second base during the Gamecocks' victory against Clemson at Fluor Field in Greenville on March 6, 2010. Morales provided much-needed vocal leadership to the team. *Courtesy of Juan Blas/TheBigSpur.com.*

Ray Tanner is known for his charisma off the field and his tough-nosed, old-school style on it. The veteran coach won his 1,000th career game at Vanderbilt early in the 2010 Southeastern Conference season. *Courtesy of Juan Blas/ TheBigSpur.com.*

The Gamecocks wait at home plate for Christian Walker after the freshman first baseman hit a home run to propel the team to a Super Regional–clinching victory at Coastal Carolina on June 13, 2010. Despite two home runs in SEC play, Walker's prodigious power appeared at just the right time for the team. *Courtesy of Juan Blas/TheBigSpur.com.*

The team poses after winning the Myrtle Beach Super Regional at BB&T Coastal Field. Two one-run victories against Coastal Carolina provided the Gamecocks their first College World Series bid since 2004. South Carolina had not even been to a Super Regional since 2007. *Courtesy of Juan Blas/TheBigSpur.com.*

Junior outfielder Whit Merrifield looks up into the rainy Omaha sky during the Gamecocks' College World Series opener against Oklahoma on June 20, 2010. Two separate weather delays caused the game to last more than eight hours. *Courtesy of Juan Blas/TheBigSpur.com.*

Sophomore outfielder Jackie Bradley Jr. extends the bat to the baseball early in the team's run at the College World Series. Bradley, out early in the season with a broken bone in his right hand, hit home runs in the Gamecocks' first two games in Omaha. He led the team in average, home runs and RBIs. *Courtesy of Juan Blas/TheBigSpur.com.*

Bayler and Bridges Teal cozy up to a few South Carolina cheerleaders and their favorite mascot on the planet, Cocky, at a Gamecocks basketball game in 2009. *Courtesy of the Teal family.*

With his favorite team and his parents watching behind him, Bayler Teal throws out the first pitch before the Gamecocks host Brown on March 13, 2010. Teal was on a break from treatment at Manhattan's Sloan-Kettering Cancer Center. *Courtesy of the Teal family.*

Bayler Teal embraces his younger brother, Bridges. Bayler's affection extended to many, but none more than his brother. *Courtesy of the Teal family.*

Bayler Teal sits in a wheelchair beside his dad, Rob, in a New York subway car. As a last-ditch treatment effort, the Teals took Bayler in early 2010 to Manhattan's Sloan-Kettering Cancer Center. *Courtesy of the Teal family.*

Right: Part of a cancer survivors rally, Bayler Teal thought he had beaten cancer for a few months in 2009. But the disease returned for good by the start of 2010. *Courtesy of the Teal family.*

Below: A nurse and Bayler Teal ham it up during one of Teal's visits to Palmetto Health Children's Hospital. Many days, Teal would volunteer to go to the hospital because he enjoyed spending time with his doctors and nurses. The hospital is the state's only free-standing children's facility. *Courtesy of the Teal family.*

Adrian Morales makes a throw over to first base during the College World Series. The third baseman included, the Gamecocks finished the season ranked thirteenth in the country in fielding percentage (.975). *Courtesy of Juan Blas/TheBigSpur.com.*

Mark Calvi intently keeps an eye on his pitcher from the Rosenblatt Stadium dugout. Calvi had been maligned as the team's longtime pitching coach, but he assembled a staff in 2010 that finished with the seventh-best earned run average (3.45) in the country. *Courtesy of Juan Blas/TheBigSpur.com.*

Ray Tanner addresses reporters at Rosenblatt Stadium before the College World Series. Tanner had taken the Gamecocks to Omaha three times before, but not since 2004. In 2010, South Carolina lost its college opener for the seventh consecutive time. *Courtesy of Juan Blas/TheBigSpur.com.*

Outfielder Whit Merrifield and assistant coach Sammy Esposito bump fists after Merrifield gets on base during the College World Series. Merrifield slumped toward the end of the regular season but picked it up in Omaha. He was drafted and signed with the Kansas City Royals after the season. *Courtesy of Juan Blas/TheBigSpur.com.*

The Gamecocks welcome home Jackie Bradley Jr. after he scores the winning run in the twelfth inning against Oklahoma in the College World Series on June 24, 2010. Bradley was down to his last strike, the season's last strike, before registering the game-tying hit. In Columbia, Bayler Teal died during the eighth inning of the game. *Courtesy of Juan Blas/ TheBigSpur.com.*

Above, left: Sophomore Michael Roth prays before his start on June 25, 2010, against Clemson in the College World Series. The left-hander was making his first start in fourteen months. He pitched a complete-game three-hitter against the Tigers and then pitched five innings against UCLA in the national title series. *Courtesy of Juan Blas/TheBigSpur.com.*

Above, right: Outfielder Jackie Bradley Jr. and shortstop Bobby Haney share an embrace during the College World Series. The Gamecocks felt as if they had team chemistry, unlike past South Carolina teams as well as the other teams playing in Omaha. *Courtesy of Juan Blas/TheBigSpur.com.*

Redshirt freshman Matt Price fires a pitch during the College World Series. The closer clicked into another gear in the postseason, picking up two saves in the Super Regional and two victories in Omaha, including the national title–sealing win against UCLA. *Courtesy of Juan Blas/TheBigSpur.com.*

Shoved down the left-field line at Rosenblatt Stadium, that does not mean South Carolina's bullpen crew could not enjoy themselves. Catcher Richard Royal wears a beach ball on his head in a light moment during the College World Series. *Courtesy of Juan Blas/ TheBigSpur.com.*

Created during the Regional win against Bucknell by reserve outfielder Robert Beary, a fungo bat with a baseball taped to it, the "Avatar Spirit Stick," became the symbol of South Carolina's postseason. It was encased after the team won the national title. *Courtesy of Juan Blas/TheBigSpur.com.*

Michael Roth talks with ESPN's Erin Andrews after his dominating performance on June 25, 2010, against Clemson in the College World Series. The sophomore dedicated the win to Bayler Teal, who died the previous day. *Courtesy of Juan Blas/TheBigSpur.com.*

Blake Cooper ices his arm during his start on June 28, 2010, against UCLA in the College World Series national championship series. Cooper made three starts in ten days in Omaha, throwing three hundred pitches. Against the Bruins, he took a one-hitter into the ninth inning of a 7–1 Gamecocks victory. *Courtesy of Juan Blas/TheBigSpur.com.*

Bayler Teal, seven, did not survive to see the Gamecocks win the national title in his honor. He succumbed to cancer on June 24, 2010, at 9:32 p.m., just as his team was beginning to mount a comeback against Oklahoma in the College World Series. The team has credited Teal with inspiring it throughout the run. *Courtesy of the Teal family.*

Above: Rob Teal helps the Gamecocks hoist the national championship trophy after they defeated UCLA on June 29, 2010. Teal, his wife Risha and their son Bridges flew to Omaha to watch South Carolina play in their late son's honor. Rob Teal wore a hat with Bayler's name on it. *Courtesy of the Teal family.*

Left: Avatar Spirit Stick in hand, teammates swamp Scott Wingo after the second baseman scores the run to win the national title for the Gamecocks on June 29, 2010. Whit Merrifield's single to right field signaled the end of the College World Series's sixty-year run at Rosenblatt Stadium. *Courtesy of Juan Blas/TheBigSpur.com.*

"It was an incredible win for us," Tanner said after the game. "It was a never-give-up day."

On the same night Bayler Teal died, South Carolina had pieced together the most dramatic victory in the program's history.

"I believe things happen for a reason," sophomore pitcher Michael Roth said. "I believe there is a higher being. I believe in God. I believe there is a God and Bayler was up there with Him."

OKLAHOMA
JUNE 24, 2010, ROSENBLATT STADIUM, OMAHA, NEBRASKA

SOUTH CAROLINA 3 (50-16)

Player	ab	r	h	rbi	bb	so	po	a	lob
Evan Marzilli lf	6	1	2	0	0	1	1	0	3
Whit Merrifield rf	5	0	0	0	0	1	0	0	0
Jackie Bradley Jr. cf	6	1	1	1	0	1	5	0	0
Christian Walker 1b	5	0	3	1	0	0	8	3	1
Adam Matthews pr	0	0	0	0	0	0	0	0	0
Jeffery Jones 1b	0	0	0	0	1	0	1	0	0
Brady Thomas dh	6	0	1	1	0	2	0	0	1
Adrian Morales 3b	5	0	1	0	0	0	1	2	2
Kyle Enders c	2	0	0	0	2	1	13	3	0
Bobby Haney ss	5	0	1	0	0	1	4	4	2
Scott Wingo 2b	1	0	0	0	0	1	1	2	0
Robert Beary ph	3	1	1	0	0	1	0	0	1
Blake Cooper p	0	0	0	0	0	0	1	0	0
Michael Roth p	0	0	0	0	0	0	1	0	0
John Taylor p	0	0	0	0	0	0	0	0	0
Matt Price p	0	0	0	0	0	0	0	0	0
Ethan Carter p	0	0	0	0	0	0	0	0	0
Tyler Webb p	0	0	0	0	0	0	0	1	0
Totals	44	3	10	3	3	9	36	15	10

OKLAHOMA 2 (50-18)

Player	ab	r	h	rbi	bb	so	po	a	lob
Chris Ellison cf	4	0	0	0	0	1	4	0	0
Max White lf	5	0	1	0	0	2	2	0	0
Garrett Buechele 3b	5	0	1	0	0	4	2	1	0
Tyler Ogle c	3	2	2	1	1	0	9	1	0
Cody Reine rf	3	0	0	0	0	2	3	0	2
Cameron Seitzer 1b	4	0	0	0	1	0	10	2	2
Caleb Bushyhead ss	5	0	1	1	0	0	3	3	0
Danny Black 2b	5	0	0	0	0	3	1	3	2
Kaleb Herren dh	3	0	0	0	0	2	0	0	0
Ricky Eisenberg ph	1	0	0	0	0	0	0	0	0
Zach Neal p	0	0	0	0	0	0	1	0	0
Jeremy Erben p	0	0	0	0	0	0	0	0	0
Ryan Duke p	0	0	0	0	0	0	0	0	0
Totals	38	2	5	2	2	14	35	10	6

Score by Innings					R H E
Oklahoma	001	010	000	001	-2 5 2
South Carolina	000	000	010	002	-3 10 1

Note: 2 outs, 2 runners LOB when the game ended.

E—Buechele (6); Ogle (4); Walker (10). DP—SC 2. LOB—OU 6; SC 12. 2B—Marzilli (8); Haney (9). HR—Ogle (12). HBP—Ellison; Reine 2; Wingo. SH—Ogle (6); Merrifield (15); Enders (7). SB—Bushyhead (14); Marzilli (7); Beary (4). CS—Ellison (5).

The University of South Carolina Baseball Team's Journey to the 2010 NCAA Championship

South Carolina	ip	h	r	er	bb	so	ab	bf	np
Blake Cooper	5.2	4	1	1	2	6	18	22	98
Michael Roth	1.1	0	0	0	0	1	4	4	13
John Taylor	1.0	0	0	0	0	1	3	3	11
Matt Price	3.0	0	0	0	0	5	9	10	50
Ethan Carter	0.0	1	1	1	0	0	1	1	2
Tyler Webb	1.0	0	0	0	0	1	3	4	13

Oklahoma	ip	h	r	er	bb	so	ab	bf	np
Zach Neal	7.0	5	1	1	1	7	25	28	104
Jeremy Erben	4.0	2	0	0	1	1	14	16	50
Ryan Duke	0.2	3	2	2	1	1	5	6	23

Win—Webb (3-2). Loss—Duke, R. (3-2). Save—None.

HBP—by Cooper (Ellison); by Neal (Wingo); by Price (Reine); by Webb (Reine). Inherited runners/scored: Erben 1/1; Roth 2/0.

Umpires—HP: A.J. Lostaglio; 1B: Paul Guillie; 2B: Kelly Gonzales; 3B: David Savage
Start: 6:09 p.m. Time: 3:47 Attendance: 2,418

Game notes
Elimination game for both teams.

Chapter 16
THROWING CURVEBALLS

JUNE 25, 2010

J ust before South Carolina sophomore Michael Roth took the mound the
following day against Clemson, he doffed his cap and held it against his
heart. Roth took the next thirty seconds to pray. He thanked God for the
opportunity to pitch, and he prayed specifically for the Teal family.

Roth also asked for a little help.

"I couldn't have pitched that game by myself," Roth said. "I definitely
think God was helping me out—and Bayler was there. He was an inspiration,
continually fighting."

Even in the extra innings against Oklahoma, Mark Calvi was thinking of
who he wanted to start the next day against rival Clemson. After the twelfth-
inning rally against the Sooners, someone mentioned to Roth that he might
be an option. Roth looked at outfielder Adam Matthews, who was beside
him on the bus, and they started to laugh.

"We thought, 'There's no way in hell they're going to let me start in
Omaha,'" Roth said. "'That's the biggest joke I've ever heard.'"

When the team got back to the hotel, the coaches agonized about the
pitching decision, as if they were negotiating a peace treaty. Eventually
they arrived at their decision, and Calvi went to inform the choice. Calvi
rehearsed his speech on the way.

The University of South Carolina Baseball Team's Journey
to the 2010 NCAA Championship

He opened the door to find Roth mesmerized by his television. Undeterred, Calvi told Roth that he was going to be the guy Friday night against Clemson. Roth sort of nodded along, but the information was not getting to him. Calvi craned his neck to see what was so fascinating on TV. It was a documentary—on sex.

"He's a guy who doesn't get caught up in the moment," senior pitching captain Jay Brown said. "Everything is the same to him. He's unlike any teammate I've been on a team with."

Despite Calvi's visit, Roth went to bed in denial about starting against Clemson. He woke up with the same feeling.

He had his reasons. Roth had started two games in his college career and both came the previous season, when he was a freshman. His first start, against Georgia Southern, lasted two innings and was little more than a glorified relief effort. Roth's second start, against College of Charleston, lasted 4 1/3 innings, but he allowed six runs on nine hits. That was on April 14, 2009—fourteen months prior to Omaha.

When the Gamecocks arrived for the College World Series, Roth had thrown just twenty-four innings in 2010. In twenty-one of his thirty-three appearances, Roth had pitched less than an inning. He was brought in as a specialist, to face one or two left-handed batters. Roth would pout when the coaches would come to retrieve him. It was like a mom calling in her son for dinner. Like the son would beg for five more minutes to play, Roth would plead for one more batter.

They gave him that chance against Bucknell in the Regional opener. Roth went 3 1/3 innings, by far his longest outing of the year, without allowing a hit. That opened the coaches' eyes.

He had pitched 2 1/3 scoreless innings in Omaha, including 1 1/3 perfect innings the day before against Oklahoma. Roth was pitching well. But starting a College World Series game? Against Clemson?

"I just figured that, at the last minute, Coach Tanner would be like, 'No, no. No, there's no way I'm letting him go out there,'" Roth said.

Calvi, though, told a Columbia radio station Friday morning that Roth was starting. Roth's cellphone started to light up with calls and texts wishing him luck. He was confused. Reality registered with Roth just before he boarded the bus to Rosenblatt Stadium. On the elevator, Tanner asked Roth how many innings he had in him.

"How should I know?" Roth told him. "I don't know. I'll throw until my arm falls off."

"What is that, one inning?" Tanner said, being a smart aleck. "Seriously, how many innings?"

"I don't know," Roth said. "Five? Six? That's what I'm shooting for."

Roth, a Greenville native, was recruited to be a power-hitting first baseman. Tanner was hopeful that Roth would help fill the huge hole left by MLB first-rounder Justin Smoak. Most of Roth's work his freshman year was geared to make him a better first baseman, a better hitter. But he hit .154 in thirteen at-bats as a freshman. Roth was not hacking it as a position player.

Roth was left-handed and had pitched some in high school; therefore, he was a natural candidate to become a project for Calvi. Including those two starts, Roth had a 4.22 ERA in thirty-two innings. A gaping hole in his pitching ability held him back: despite being a lefty, he could not get out left-handed batters.

Roth was not deceptive. He threw over the top. His fastball topped out at eighty-five miles an hour. His breaking pitches did not move all that much. There was nothing to disguise his motion. Roth was throwing batting practice.

Something occurred to Calvi one day as he watched Roth take fielding practice at first base. When Roth threw to second base to begin double plays, his sidearm delivery to the bag was hard and accurate. Calvi wondered if Roth could translate that to the mound. He asked Roth if he would consider it.

"I thought, 'Why would I?'" Roth said. "'No, that's stupid.'"

Calvi told him to try it anyway.

"I hated it," Roth said. "I was pissed. It was the running joke around our staff."

In the spring, though, the delivery started to come around. Roth would throw from a three-quarter arm angle against lefties. He still threw over the top to right-handed batters. He started getting both out consistently.

That's why Roth got the ball against Clemson, which featured six left-handed batters in the lineup.

The University of South Carolina Baseball Team's Journey to the 2010 NCAA Championship

Roth is as smart as he is silly. The Gamecocks had the highest grade-point average, a 3.12, of any team in the College World Series. An international business major in the nationally regarded Darla Moore School of Business, Roth had the highest GPA of any player on the team, a 3.82.

Roth is a thinker, an analyzer. That's true of most lefties. So Roth spent the short ride from the downtown hotel to the stadium in thought. It led him to the conclusion that he would approach the start no differently than his relief appearances. After all, he had a 1.37 ERA. He would stick with his routine, even if it was a bit unorthodox.

When the Gamecocks took batting practice, Roth, who had nine at-bats all year, was in the cage. Then he was at first base, fielding ground balls from Calvi's fungo. That's what he did before every game all season. That's what he was going to do before starting in the College World Series.

Roth and Calvi were laughing about it. Adrian Morales wasn't. He fumed. To him, Roth was making a mockery of the game. He didn't think Roth was taking the start seriously enough.

"He was like, 'This kid's an idiot,'" Roth said.

Roth threw on the side to get loose, stretched with some elastic bands—warm-up drills he engaged in before every game—and then he went to the mound. "I took it like I was relieving in the first inning," Roth said.

The presumption in Omaha was that Roth would give South Carolina two, maybe three innings. Tanner said five was his "dream scenario."

"Ray Tanner's not asking Michael Roth to go out and throw a complete game," ESPN's Robin Ventura said at the top of the broadcast.

If the Tigers made it as easy on Roth as they did in the first inning, he would have a shot at going the distance. Chris Epps grounded the first pitch of the game to Scott Wingo at second base. Two more ground balls, to short and third, and Roth needed just five more tosses to get Clemson 1-2-3 in the first. Roth was throwing fielding practice.

Kyle Parker, one of the rare right-handed hitters in the Clemson lineup, walked to begin the second. But Brad Miller struck out (on a seventy-four-mile-an-hour breaking ball), and John Hinson lined into a double play, with Parker on the move. Roth had made it through his two innings, and he would not walk another Tiger.

Clemson scored its first—and only—run in the third. It required a leadoff double from Richie Shaffer, consecutive ground balls and a passed ball. Meanwhile, the Gamecocks scored a run in each of the first four innings and five of the first six to support Roth, who got stronger and stronger as the game progressed.

Tanner's dream scenario of five innings came and went. Roth was still on the mound.

"You get to five, you've had a day," Tanner said. "It wasn't that I didn't believe in him or I was being cautious. I was realistic. You're asking a guy to do something that he hasn't done. What he had done was be a good reliever for us. Sometimes that was a batter, an inning, maybe two innings."

When the Gamecocks batted, Roth didn't sit by himself in solitude. He didn't act as if he had a no-hitter going. He yukked it up with his teammates.

"I think he decided he was going to be Michael Roth and he was going to have fun no matter what," Holbrook said. "If you had to rank people on our team in terms of their zest for life, he's probably numero uno. You know, he loves life."

The only thing Roth consciously did between innings was avoid Calvi and Tanner. For fear of coming out, he got even better. Roth was perfect in the sixth and seventh innings. Three of Roth's sixteen ground-ball outs came in a seven-pitch seventh. It was at that point that the ninth, and a complete game, started to come into view. Down 5–1, the Tigers were having worse and worse at-bats. They appeared to concede the game. They figured they could rebound against the Gamecocks the next night.

Roth had given up one hit through seven innings.

"They didn't make a single adjustment," Roth said. "I just kept throwing fastballs inside, and they just kept getting on the plate. That's their problem."

Roth allowed a single in the eighth and ninth innings, but Clemson had no base runners past second after it scored in the third. Tigers left-handed hitters were 0 for 20 against Roth until a Miller single in the ninth. He struck out Clemson's hottest hitters, Parker and Hinson, for the final two outs.

Roth had thrown a three-hit complete game against Clemson in the College World Series. A left-handed specialist had pitched just the second complete game in Omaha since 2006. The Gamecocks were one win from the national championship series.

"It had to be certainly one of the most clutch pitching performances that I've ever been associated with," Tanner said. "Many people have said in Omaha that it's one of the best-pitched games in the history of the College World Series."

The University of South Carolina Baseball Team's Journey to the 2010 NCAA Championship

CLEMSON
JUNE 25, 2010, ROSENBLATT STADIUM, OMAHA, NEBRASKA

SOUTH CAROLINA 5 (51-16)

Player	ab	r	h	rbi	bb	so	po	a	lob
Evan Marzilli lf	2	2	1	0	2	1	1	0	0
Whit Merrifield rf	4	0	0	0	0	1	2	0	0
Jackie Bradley Jr. cf	3	0	1	2	1	0	0	0	1
Christian Walker 1b	4	0	1	0	0	0	13	1	1
Brady Thomas dh	4	2	2	0	0	0	0	0	0
Adrian Morales 3b	4	0	1	1	0	0	2	4	0
Kyle Enders c	4	1	2	2	0	0	5	0	0
Bobby Haney ss	3	0	0	0	1	0	0	5	1
Scott Wingo 2b	4	0	0	0	0	1	3	4	1
Michael Roth p	0	0	0	0	0	0	1	1	0
Totals	**32**	**5**	**8**	**5**	**4**	**3**	**27**	**15**	**4**

CLEMSON 1 (45-24)

Player	ab	r	h	rbi	bb	so	po	a	lob
Chris Epps dh	2	0	0	0	0	1	0	0	0
John Nester ph/dh	2	0	0	0	0	0	0	0	0
Mike Freeman 2b	4	0	0	0	0	0	2	5	2
Jeff Schaus lf	4	0	0	0	0	0	1	0	0
Kyle Parker rf	2	0	0	0	1	1	3	1	0
Brad Miller ss	4	0	1	0	0	1	4	4	1
John Hinson 3b	4	0	0	0	0	1	0	0	1
Richie Shaffer 1b	2	1	1	0	0	0	10	1	0
Wilson Boyd cf	3	0	0	0	0	0	4	0	0
Spencer Kieboom c	3	0	0	0	0	0	4	0	0
Phil Pohl c	3	0	1	0	0	0	3	1	1
Dominic Leone p	0	0	0	0	0	0	0	0	0
David Haselden p	0	0	0	0	0	0	0	0	0
Tomas Cruz p	0	0	0	0	0	0	0	1	0
Totals	**33**	**1**	**3**	**0**	**1**	**4**	**31**	**12**	**6**

Score by Innings				R H E
South Carolina	111	101	000	- 5 8 1
Clemson	001	000	000	- 1 3 0

E—Wingo (9). DP—SC 1; CU 2. LOB—SC 4; CU 5. 2B—Marzilli (8); Bradley (12); Thomas (13); Shaffer (11). HR—Enders (3). HBP—Parker; Shaffer. SB—Marzilli (7).

South Carolina	ip	h	r	er	bb	so	ab	bf	np
Michael Roth	9	3	1	1	1	4	30	33	108

Clemson	ip	h	r	er	bb	so	ab	bf	np
Dominic Leone	2.2	4	3	3	1	0	11	12	44
David Haselden	3.1	4	2	2	1	0	13	14	46
Tomas Cruz	3.0	0	0	0	2	3	8	10	39

Win—Roth (2-1). Loss—Leone (3-2). Save—None.
HBP—by Roth (Parker); by Roth (Shaffer). PB—Enders (10).

Umpires—HP: Gus Rodriguez; 1B: Jim Jackson; 2B: Chris Coskey; 3B: Mark Ditsworth
Start: 8:10 p.m.   Time 2:22   Attendance: 22,194

Game notes
Elimination game for South Carolina.

Chapter 17

TAMING TIGERS

JUNE 26, 2010

S outh Carolina had to defeat Clemson twice to play for the national championship. It was something that had worked out well before. The Gamecocks did it in 2002.

Knowing that gave the 2010 Gamecocks confidence. Knowing Clemson's lineup and pitching staff did, too. The Gamecocks wanted to see the Tigers in the College World Series. They liked their chances against them, even if Clemson had destroyed South Carolina 19–6 in the teams' most recent meeting in March.

"I think us getting beat 19–6 is the best thing that happened to us," said Gamecocks second baseman Scott Wingo, whose dad had played baseball at Clemson. "I think we were a little bit fired up about that. We wanted to get payback."

Halfway there after Michael Roth's three-hitter Friday night, the Gamecocks finished the job Saturday. Enigmatic starter Sam Dyson, despite a 6-5 record and a career 4.61 ERA, gave up just two runs in 6 2/3 innings. A 2–2 game in the seventh, Christian Walker and Adrian Morales provided consecutive RBI singles to give South Carolina a 4–2 lead. Walker, on his way to hitting .424 (12 of 29) in Omaha, admitted he was motivated by the fact that Clemson walked Jackie Bradley Jr. to get to him.

Closer Matt Price allowed a run in the eighth but went the final 2 1/3 innings to get his fourth win of the season. With the 4–3 victory against the Tigers, South Carolina had pulled off a repeat of 2002.

The Gamecocks had won four games in five days to stave off elimination and play for the national title.

"It's really been incredible," Ray Tanner said after the game. "It really has."

Unlike 2002, South Carolina would have three chances to win two games for the first major national championship in school history. UCLA was the only thing that stood in the way.

"We didn't want to just get here," right fielder Whit Merrifield said that Saturday night. "We wanted to do something here. And we're in the position now to do something that this program has never accomplished before."

First, though, the Gamecocks engaged in one of their Omaha traditions. The ten-minute postgame bus rides from Rosenblatt Stadium to the team's hotel had become epic. After every one of the Gamecocks' four elimination-game wins that week, the bus was the first chance they had to wrap their brains around what just happened.

"We would be like, 'How did we just win that game?'" Roth said. "'We're not even that good. How did we win?'"

The Gamecocks created a soundtrack to go with the experience. As the bus pulled out of the stadium parking lot, the national anthem was the playlist's standard first song. The mandatory second selection was "Silent Night"—a natural choice for Omaha in June.

Then it was an open mic. Someone, whoever, would start with a line, and then the rest of the Gamecocks' glee club would join. One night, it was Flo Rida's "Boots with the Fur." Another, it was Brian McKnight's "One." There were also several Justin Bieber fans on the team.

All the while, Morales wore a tense look on his face. He hated it.

"Dude, shut up, man," he would say, scolding the team. "We haven't won anything yet."

The Gamecocks kept singing.

The joy the Gamecocks were playing with was just as obvious back in South Carolina as it was on that bus in Omaha. And that meant a lot to fans who had suffered through so many of the athletic program's heartbreaks. Win or lose in the national title series, this was already something South Carolina fans could celebrate. Heck, to them, beating Clemson in any major sport was worth a parade in Columbia.

Rob Teal was one of those proud fans. When he was in high school, the Bishopville newspaper named the biggest Clemson and South Carolina fans in Lee County. Teal was the Gamecocks' representative. As a father, Rob was intent on putting that South Carolina spirit into his two boys. It was a process. The first time the baseball team came to visit Bayler in the hospital, when he was five, he was only excited because his dad was excited. But as he got older, Bayler's own love for the Gamecocks took hold.

It remained that way until he died during the College World Series run South Carolina had dedicated to him. The Gamecocks then played in his memory, Roth and other players writing "BT" on their hats, gloves and bats.

In Bishopville, the community descended on the Teals' home after Bayler's death. Wave after wave of people came over, often bringing a dish or two, to show sympathy and support. Naturally, the College World Series was on in the house. Friday night, someone in the room noticed the "BT" on Roth's cap.

"I thought, 'What's that?'" said Risha Teal, Bayler's mom. "I just couldn't believe they would do that. I couldn't believe that was about our son."

Smiles and tears filled the room. They continued to do so as Roth willed himself through inning after inning. Afterward, when Roth brought up Bayler in the postgame interview on ESPN, the room broke down again. Half a country away, Bayler's spirit was still alive and well. Even though it was over, his life still meant something powerful.

The following day at Bayler's visitation, friends and family buzzed about what the Gamecocks were doing in Omaha—and doing for Bayler. The pain of Bayler losing his life was still very real, very present, but there was something else trumping that pain. Instead of dwelling in the sadness of those days, there was something positive to talk about. And it related directly to Bayler.

Bayler's favorite nurse at Palmetto Health Children's Hospital, Kimberly Boland, gave Bayler a fitting tribute. When she got to his casket, she attached something to his jacket. It was a small, garnet sticker.

It said, "Beat Clemson."

As much as the Teals love their hometown, it was suffocating them. They had barely caught a breath since Bayler died on Thursday night. With their house full, Rob and Risha jumped in the car a few times and drove around town just to temporarily escape. On one of those rides, Rob brought up the idea of going to Omaha for the national championship series.

Rob eventually found a suitable deal that would take the Teals, including five-year-old Bridges, from Charlotte to Omaha, via Dallas. If the Gamecocks were going to play for Bayler, and especially if they were going to win for him, the Teals wanted to be there.

If anyone deserved a problem-free travel day, it was the Teals. But summer storms did not cooperate. Rob, Risha and Bridges arrived in Charlotte on Monday morning only to learn their flight had been canceled. Their rescheduled flight would arrive in Omaha that night, but not in time to make the first game against UCLA.

But about 3:00 p.m., Rob got a call informing him that a charter flight had been arranged for the family. It would get the Teals to Omaha in time for the game.

Ashley Gilfillan, a Columbia-area real estate agent, had been following Bayler's story. Gilfillan heard about the family's canceled flight. With three kids of his own, he put himself in the Teals' position. He wanted to help. Gilfillan called a friend, John Denise, who works with a charter service that shuttles professional golfers around the country.

Denise told him he would put in a call to a Charlotte-based crew but not to get his hopes up. The charter company typically asks for twenty-four hours' notice before a flight to prepare the plane and line up a crew. The minimum is eight hours' notice.

At first, Charlotte said no way. The window was too tight. Denise continued to plead, saying he was calling in a favor on this one. Charlotte radioed a pilot that had just landed and told him there was a "pop-up trip." He told the pilot to bring the plane in but not to shut it down. A van was then sent to retrieve the Teals from the main terminal. Often, Denise said, even celebrities and millionaires blow off charter companies, leaving them in the lurch. To that end, very little is done without the proper paperwork completed. But no one asked the Teals to sign a thing.

"We kind of did everything backward," Denise said.

They did it quickly, too. Less than an hour after the idea was introduced to Denise, the flight was in the air. It was easily the fastest Denise had seen a charter get its wheels up in his seven-plus years working in aviation.

In the frenetic hour that preceded takeoff, several obstacles nearly nixed the flight. Bad weather grounded their commercial flight, but the charter plane was still cleared because it would fly at a higher altitude.

The University of South Carolina Baseball Team's Journey
to the 2010 NCAA Championship

Fuel range was also an issue. Because the plane had just landed from another trip, it did not have a full tank. Charter planes are federally required to carry a minimum fuel reserve, and the trip from Charlotte to Omaha would flirt with the minimum. If the plane had to stop somewhere along the way to refuel, that would have caused the pilot to exceed his ten-hour daily limit in the cockpit—and cause the Teals to miss the game.

The fuel quandary boiled down to Denise estimating how much Rob, Risha and Bridges weighed. The math worked—barely. If anyone else had gone with them, the plane would have had to stop for fuel. If Bridges were an adult, the plane would have had to stop for fuel. A gentler-than-normal headwind also worked in the Teals' favor.

"I attribute everything to divine intervention," Denise said.

Gilfillan was the catalyst. He put down more than $10,000 for the flight. Fans' donations and a contribution from Tanner allowed him to pay off the balance. Still, Gilfillan risked a large sum of money for the happiness of strangers.

The Teals arrived in Omaha just as the game was beginning. The charter service had a rental car waiting for them on the tarmac. Rob, Risha and Bridges got in to find the radio had been set to the game. Treated like royalty, the Teals headed for Rosenblatt Stadium.

With Bayler's help, Rob was confident what the outcome there would be. "We've never won a national championship in any sport that matters," he said then. "If I had money to bet, I'd bet we'll win this thing. I've got this feeling."

The players had the same feeling, for the very same reason. "When he passed, we felt like we had something behind us then. We thought that we weren't going to lose," said Merrifield, Bayler's favorite player. "It went from us playing to win to us thinking we weren't going to lose. We just weren't. It's hard to explain. Things were going to go our way."

CLEMSON
JUNE 26, 2010, ROSENBLATT STADIUM, OMAHA, NEBRASKA

SOUTH CAROLINA 4 (52-16)

Player	ab	r	h	rbi	bb	so	po	a	lob
Evan Marzilli lf	3	2	1	0	1	0	1	0	0
Whit Merrifield rf	5	0	3	0	0	1	1	0	1
Jackie Bradley Jr. cf	2	1	1	0	1	0	2	0	1
Christian Walker 1b	4	1	2	2	0	0	12	0	1
Adrian Morales 3b	4	0	1	1	0	1	0	2	1
Adam Matthews dh	3	0	0	0	0	1	0	0	0
Brady Thomas ph/dh	0	0	0	0	1	0	0	0	0
Kyle Enders c	4	0	0	0	0	2	8	0	3
Bobby Haney ss	4	0	1	0	0	1	1	3	1
Scott Wingo 2b	3	0	0	0	1	0	2	7	2
Sam Dyson p	0	0	0	0	0	0	0	0	0
Matt Price p	0	0	0	0	0	0	0	0	0
Totals	**32**	**4**	**9**	**3**	**4**	**6**	**27**	**12**	**10**

CLEMSON 3 (45-25)

Player	ab	r	h	rbi	bb	so	po	a	lob
Will Lamb dh	4	1	1	0	0	0	0	0	0
Mike Freeman 2b	5	0	2	0	0	1	3	2	0
Jeff Schaus lf	5	0	1	1	0	1	0	0	1
Kyle Parker rf	3	0	0	0	0	2	1	0	2
John Hinson 3b	3	1	2	0	1	1	0	2	2
Brad Miller ss	4	0	0	1	0	0	2	3	0
Richie Shaffer 1b	4	0	1	0	0	1	9	0	1
Wilson Boyd cf	4	0	1	0	0	1	4	0	2
Spencer Kieboom c	2	0	0	0	0	0	4	2	1
Chris Epps ph	0	1	0	0	1	0	0	0	0
John Nester c	1	0	0	0	0	1	1	0	0
Casey Harman p	0	0	0	0	0	0	0	2	0
Alex Frederick p	0	0	0	0	0	0	0	0	0
Scott Weismann p	0	0	0	0	0	0	0	0	0
Kevin Brady p	0	0	0	0	0	0	0	0	0
Totals	**35**	**3**	**8**	**2**	**2**	**8**	**24**	**11**	**9**

The University of South Carolina Baseball Team's Journey to the 2010 NCAA Championship

Score by Innings				R H E
Clemson	001	000	110	- 3 8 3
South Carolina	100	100	20X	- 4 9 1

E—Miller (32); Kieboom (1); Nester (7); Wingo (10). DP—CU 2. LOB—CU 9; SC 10. 2B—Merrifield (12). 3B—Hinson (1); Merrifield (1). HR—Walker (9). HBP—Lamb; Parker; Marzilli; Bradley. SB—Marzilli (8); Matthews (6).

South Carolina	ip	h	r	er	bb	so	ab	bf	np
Sam Dyson	6.2	5	2	2	2	5	25	29	111
Matt Price	2.1	3	1	1	0	3	10	10	41

Clemson	ip	h	r	er	bb	so	ab	bf	np
Casey Harman	6.1	7	3	3	0	5	26	28	102
Alex Frederick	0.2	2	1	1	2	1	4	6	28
Scott Weismann	0.1	0	0	0	2	0	1	3	13
Kevin Brady	0.2	0	0	0	0	0	1	1	3

Win—Price (4-1). Loss—Harman (8-4). Save—None.
HBP—by Dyson (Lamb); by Dyson (Parker); by Harman (Bradley); by Harman (Marzilli). PB—Enders (11).

Umpires—HP: Kelly Gonzales; 1B: David Savage; 2B: A.J. Lostaglio; 3B: Paul Guillie
Start: 6:09 p.m.   Time: 3:04   Attendance: 12,593

Game notes
Elimination game for both teams.

Chapter 18

NEARING HISTORY

JUNE 28, 2010

The Teals made it to their seats at Rosenblatt Stadium in the second inning. ESPN's cameras found them almost immediately. So did South Carolina assistant coach Chad Holbrook, who had been monitoring their journey all afternoon.

Holbrook had been to the national championship series with North Carolina in 2006 and 2007. But South Carolina's run that week had been about much more than baseball. The thirty-nine-year-old was connected to the Teals in a way far too many families understand. And Holbrook had brought them into the Gamecocks' fold.

Even though he had a beyond reasonable excuse, missing Bayler's funeral—and those final few days—ate at Holbrook. So looking into the stands and seeing Rob, Risha and Bridges had a calming effect.

"It was comforting to know they were going to be at the game," he said. "We were on the brink of doing something pretty special, but that immediately disappeared. Seeing their faces, seeing Bayler's brother, that's what meant the most. I went numb."

Holbrook wasn't the only one in a Gamecock uniform who felt Bayler's impact. The tone of second baseman Scott Wingo's pregame stories had changed. He wasn't shocking teammates anymore. He wasn't making them laugh. He talked before the Clemson and UCLA games about winning for Bayler.

"Bayler was a big part of this program. It was sad for us," said senior pitcher Jay Brown, among the players closest to the Teals. "We were just playing baseball. There's so much more to this world, and life, than the game of baseball. It really puts it into perspective and makes you appreciate what you have."

Cory Whitaker and his family make the trip from Van Alstyne, Texas, to Omaha every summer for the College World Series. And every summer the Whitakers, like a lot of nonpartisan fans at Rosenblatt Stadium, adopt a team.

Whitaker knew South Carolina was his team after watching Michael Roth deliver his complete game against Clemson—and then dedicate the performance to Bayler. His only preexisting connection to the Palmetto State the fact that his aunt lives in Aiken, Whitaker even went so far as to have a T-shirt made to support the Gamecocks. The black shirt had "WIN IT 4 BT" stitched on the front in white lettering.

With its heart-pounding, inspiring week, South Carolina had become Omaha's team. It had become America's team. Clemson fans even admitted that Bayler's story had them pulling for the Gamecocks to win the title.

UCLA, though, was not rooting for South Carolina. And its pitching made it a strong favorite in the series. The Bruins' three starters had thirty-four combined victories; a reliever had just become the Gamecocks' third starter. The Bruins were second in the country with a 3.01 ERA; South Carolina's was a half-run higher, even though pitching had carried the team.

"They've got some arms," Gamecocks outfielder Jackie Bradley Jr. said the day before the series, "I'll tell you that."

UCLA ace Gerrit Cole (11-3, 2.87 ERA) was a first-round pick out of high school who turned down the New York Yankees for college ball. At six feet, four inches and 220 pounds, he was a bear of a Bruin. Gamecocks coach Ray Tanner compared Cole to Roger Clemens. Coming in, Cole had 151 strikeouts in 116 innings, an average of 1.3 an inning.

South Carolina's resident David, Blake Cooper, was the choice to oppose Cole. But Cooper's right arm had already slung 164 stones in Omaha. He had thrown 67 pitches in five innings in the opener against Oklahoma, coming out only because of the weather delay. He came back on three days' rest and threw 98 pitches in 5 2/3 innings in the 12-inning win against Oklahoma.

Tanner asked Cooper, the senior, when he would like to make his final college start. He could have the ball against the Bruins in game one or game two. It was his call. Cooper said it didn't matter. Tired was tired. He might as well go Monday. He wouldn't feel any differently Tuesday.

"He just wanted me to get through five or six innings," Cooper said, "to give us a chance."

Cooper normally did long toss across the field to warm up his arm, but he could only throw from ninety feet before game one. He could tell the velocity on his fastball was down at least five miles an hour.

"I don't have much in the tank," Cooper told pitching coach Mark Calvi. Calvi sternly told him to dig deep.

Rob is still convinced Bayler was playing a video game with South Carolina and UCLA that night. The Gamecocks got every bounce in the game, and there were a lot of them. "South Carolina doesn't get breaks like that—ever," he said. "It goes the other way."

In the first inning, the Gamecocks scored their first run as a result of three singles—a bunt, a bloop and a check-swing. With two outs, Adrian Morales then sent a slow roller to UCLA second baseman Cody Regis. Regis picked up his glove early, and the ball scooted through his legs and into shallow right-center field. The error plated another run for South Carolina. Regis was only playing the position because the team's regular second baseman broke his wrist in the post–Super Regional dog pile.

"You can't explain stuff like that," right fielder Whit Merrifield said, "and it kept happening over and over again."

Baylerball was in effect.

A chopper went under the UCLA first baseman's glove in the third. Cole botched a bunt later in that inning. No. 8 hitter Bobby Haney, without an RBI in the College World Series, then drove in two runs with two outs.

Cole looked mystified on the mound. He gave up one or two hard-hit balls, but the Gamecocks led 5–0 by the top of the third. Cole allowed six runs on ten hits—both career highs—in the first five innings. They might not have been mashing the ball, but UCLA coach John Savage said the Gamecocks deserved credit for making contact against his starter. No. 3 in the country in strikeouts, it took Cole twenty-nine batters to register his first "K." He finished with two strikeouts after thirteen in his previous start.

It was a party in the Gamecocks' dugout, even when things did not go to perfection. When Wingo botched a couple of plays in the first inning, his teammates peppered him with jokes. A little later, when he made a short flip to first base—nearly running it all the way to the bag to avoid a throw—they broke out in applause as if he had just won the game for them. "I made a play a grandma could make, and they started going crazy," Wingo said. "All you can do is laugh."

ESPN cameras showed Roth doing plenty of that in the dugout. He was flanked by Nick Ebert, who wore eye black all over his face and had a Mohawk haircut that he called an "Omahawk." Patrick Sullivan, clutching the Avatar Spirit Stick, was beside them.

The Gamecocks were far from a juggernaut—and they were a bit on the strange side—but the sum of their parts added up to something special in Omaha.

"They were able to pull together instead of standing alone," Tanner said. "I'm not going to sit here and tell you, 'All this was working. I knew we were going to win a national championship.' I'm not telling you that. But, as a coach, when you see a lot of positive things happening, you think you have a chance. Not necessarily to win a national championship, but you think you have a chance to win that day, have a good week, win a series. You think you're putting the pieces in place."

South Carolina had six runs on the board by the time Cooper gave up his first hit with one out in the fifth inning. He hit ninety miles an hour a couple of times, but his fastball was in the low eighties most of the night. Cooper leaned heavily on his curveball and slider, making UCLA hitters look foolish with them. Even though Cooper's arm angle sagged lower and lower—a mechanical flaw that would wreck most pitchers' outings—he was still highly accurate and efficient. UCLA had no idea that Cooper was pitching at 50 percent—if that. He looked like an All-American to the Bruins. Cooper had them fooled. He finished the game with ten strikeouts, topping double digits for just the third time in his career. He did it with a bunch of smoke, mirrors and a floating slider.

"The best ones don't have to be 100 percent to beat you," Calvi said. "The best ones take whatever they've got and make it into 100 percent. He said, 'I'm going to take what I have and I'm going to beat their ass with what I have.'"

In the bottom of the eighth, South Carolina's sports information director for baseball, Andrew Kitick, scurried around the press box to inform reporters that all nine Gamecocks had at least one hit. At that point, Cooper had allowed one hit. He left in the ninth inning, having thrown exactly three hundred pitches in the College World Series. He had taken down one last giant.

The country boy from Neeses wanted to be considered one of the best pitchers in South Carolina history. His three starts in nine days in Omaha sealed that.

"Legendary. That kid pitched his way into the record books," Calvi said. "Not just South Carolina, but college baseball."

After John Taylor finished out a 7–1 Gamecocks victory, the Teals made their way down to the field. The first thing they did was find Holbrook and his wife, Jennifer. One family had vanquished cancer. The other had not been so fortunate. The two mothers held on to one another for five minutes. Chad, weeping, apologized for missing the funeral. Rob told him that was completely unnecessary, considering what he was doing and where he was.

"It was not important," Holbrook said. "It was not important we were one win away from a national championship."

Several of the players met the Teals for the first time after the game. Whatever inspiration South Carolina had playing for Bayler was only enhanced by seeing Rob, Risha and Bridges.

"His dad was convinced we were going to win," Roth said. "He said, 'Y'all are going to win, and Bayler's going to help.'"

UCLA
June 28, 2010, Rosenblatt Stadium, Omaha, Nebraska

South Carolina 7 (53-16)

Player	ab	r	h	rbi	bb	so	po	a	lob
Evan Marzilli lf	4	0	2	1	1	0	1	0	0
Whit Merrifield rf	5	0	1	1	0	1	1	0	0
Jackie Bradley Jr. cf	5	1	2	0	0	1	1	0	4
Christian Walker 1b	5	1	2	0	0	0	10	0	1
Brady Thomas dh	3	1	1	1	0	0	0	0	0
Adam Matthews ph	1	0	1	0	0	0	0	0	0
Adrian Morales 3b	5	2	1	0	0	0	0	0	0
Kyle Enders c	5	0	1	0	0	0	10	0	3
Bobby Haney ss	3	0	2	3	0	0	1	3	0
Scott Wingo 2b	4	2	1	0	0	0	2	6	1
Blake Cooper p	0	0	0	0	0	0	1	2	0
John Taylor p	0	0	0	0	0	0	0	0	0
Totals	**40**	**7**	**14**	**6**	**1**	**2**	**27**	**11**	**9**

UCLA 1 (51-16)

Player	ab	r	h	rbi	bb	so	po	a	lob
Beau Amaral cf	4	0	0	0	0	0	4	0	0
Niko Gallego ss	4	0	0	0	0	3	2	3	1
Cody Regis 2b	4	1	1	0	0	1	0	1	2
Blair Dunlap dh	3	0	0	0	0	2	0	0	1
Marc Navarro dh	0	0	0	0	1	0	0	0	0
Jeff Gelalich lf	3	0	1	0	0	1	2	0	0
Dean Espy 3b	3	0	0	0	0	1	0	0	0
Trevor Brown 3b	1	0	0	0	0	0	0	0	0
Justin Uribe 1b	4	0	0	0	0	0	9	0	2
Chris Giovinazzo rf	3	0	0	0	0	1	6	4	2
Steve Rodriguez c	2	0	1	0	0	1	4	2	0
Gerrit Cole p	0	0	0	0	0	0	0	3	0
Matt Grace p	0	0	0	0	0	0	0	1	0
Scott Griggs p	0	0	0	0	0	0	0	0	0
Totals	**31**	**1**	**3**	**0**	**1**	**10**	**27**	**14**	**8**

Score by Innings				R H E
South Carolina	212	010	010	- 7 14 2
UCLA	000	000	001	- 1 3 2

E—Wingo 2 (12); Regis (12); Cole (1). DP—SC 1. LOB—SC 9; UCLA 6. 3B—Wingo (3). HBP—Gelalich; Rodriguez. SF—Haney (3). SB—Matthews (7); Wingo (2); Gelalich (7).

South Carolina	ip	h	r	er	bb	so	ab	bf	np
Blake Cooper	8.0	3	1	1	1	10	29	32	135
John Taylor	1.0	0	0	0	0	0	2	2	6

UCLA	ip	h	r	er	bb	so	ab	bf	np
Gerrit Cole	7.0	11	6	4	1	2	31	33	127
Matt Grace	1.1	3	1	1	1	0	7	8	38
Scott Griggs	0.2	0	0	0	0	1	2	2	8

Win—Cooper (13-2). Loss—Cole (11-4). Save—None.
HBP—by Cooper (Rodriguez); by Cooper (Gelalich). Cooper faced 3 batters in the 9th.

Umpires—HP: A.J. Lostaglio; 1B: Paul Guillie; 2B: Kelly Gonzales; 3B: Mark Ditsworth
Start: 6:42 p.m.   Time: 3:28   Attendance: 23,181

Game notes
Game 1 of best-of-three championship series (South Carolina leads, 1-0).

Chapter 19
CROWNING CHAMPIONS

JUNE 29, 2010

D espite taking the first game of the national championship series with ease, South Carolina still was in an enormous hole against UCLA.

As of the College World Series, UCLA had won 106 NCAA titles—more than any university in the country. The school's softball program had provided the most recent championship earlier in the month. A new trophy, or several, is welcomed to UCLA's Hall of Champions every year.

At South Carolina, there is no need for a Hall of Champions.

"I'm aware," Gamecocks coach Ray Tanner said before the series began.

South Carolina's lone NCAA title is the 2002 women's track championship. It was no doubt an accomplishment for Curtis Frye and his athletes, but it hardly registered on a local level, much less in the South or nationally. The top trophies the men's teams had secured were the 1971 ACC title in basketball and the 1969 ACC championship in football.

In 2002, Tanner's team had come within a game of winning the biggest trophy in school history. He beamed about the welcome the Gamecocks received after just getting close. He allowed himself, just for a moment, to consider what it would be like in Columbia if his 2010 team could win just one more game.

"I would like, very much, for our university to experience that," Tanner said. "I think that would be one of the greatest things that could happen."

Before his complete game against Clemson, Tanner said his "dream" for sophomore Michael Roth was five innings. That's actually what Roth gave Tanner against UCLA. The left-hander allowed a run on six hits, gutting his way through 77 pitches after throwing 108 in the three-hitter against the Tigers. Before June, the most pitches Roth had thrown in a month was 106, in May. In Omaha, he threw 185 in the span of five days. Of the 531 pitches he threw all season, 35 percent came in two outings at the College World Series. Roth had pitched 24 innings in the team's sixty-three games and three months before Omaha—and he pitched 16 1/3 innings in seven games and ten days there.

The second start came in a game that could deliver South Carolina's long-awaited championship.

"It never crossed my mind I was pitching for the national championship," said Roth, who again took batting practice and fielded grounders before the game. "If you let that into your mind, it can screw you up."

Roth left with the Gamecocks trailing 1–0. The Bruins needed an infield hit, a bunt and a single to even score the run against Roth. He started against Clemson because of the number of left-handed hitters in the Tigers' lineup. UCLA, though, had just three left-handed batters in its lineup. Mark Calvi and Tanner were riding momentum for Roth's encore. They got away with it, too.

"That shouldn't happen," said Roth, who trotted to the dugout after five innings and promptly clocked in at his second job as the team's head cheerleader.

Like the second Oklahoma game, South Carolina missed a lot of early scoring opportunities. The Gamecocks left ten runners on base in six innings against UCLA starter Rob Rasmussen. Like the second Oklahoma game, the Gamecocks finally scored their first run in the eighth inning. UCLA was foiled by another Baylerball.

Shortstop Bobby Haney sent the eighth pitch of a solid at-bat to the right side of the infield. UCLA first baseman Dean Espy moved to his right, but he briefly took his eye off the ball and it skipped off the side of his glove and into right field. Robert Beary scored easily from second to tie the game, 1–1. Espy was charged with an error, but it wasn't his biggest mistake of the inning. Upon returning to the dugout, he punched a wall and had to leave the game.

UCLA had the bases loaded with two outs in the ninth. The go-ahead run was ninety feet from home plate. After a lengthy visit from Calvi, closer Matt Price buckled Bruins shortstop Niko Gallego with an eighty-six-mile-an-hour slider—faster than Roth's best heater. Price clenched his fists and roared as he backed off the mound, emotional fuel he would need for the next two scoreless innings.

South Carolina could not end its Omaha stay any other way than extra innings. It was only logical given the team's thrill ride in the first six games at the College World Series. Still 1–1, a single swing could bring the school its first men's national championship.

Scott Wingo, 2 for 18 in Omaha, was first up in the eleventh inning. Wingo's best chance of getting on base was likely a walk—or getting hit. The junior had set the school record for that earlier in the season. In a full count, Wingo showed bunt against UCLA closer Dan Klein. He pulled the bat back in time, though, to take ball four.

The title-winning run was on first with none out and the top of the lineup coming to the plate. The first pitch to leadoff hitter Evan Marzilli glanced off the catcher's mitt and to the backstop. The passed ball moved Wingo to second. With the winning run in scoring position and none out, the energy at Rosenblatt Stadium changed. The result felt inevitable when Marzilli got down a bunt to move Wingo to third.

With one out and the national championship–clinching run ninety feet away, baseball logic dictated that UCLA would walk Whit Merrifield and Jackie Bradley Jr. and take its chances with Christian Walker, praying the slow freshman would ground into a double play. But Bruins coach John Savage did not go that route. Instead, he allowed Klein to pitch to Merrifield, who was 0 for 4 with a sacrifice and had struck out his last time up against Klein.

"It sent a little message to me that they thought they could get me out," Merrifield said. "I couldn't let that happen."

Klein missed low with a fastball to put Merrifield ahead in the at-bat, 1-0. Merrifield watched ball two run low. He had a big advantage in a 2-0 count. A fly ball would win the game. A ground ball to the right spot would win the game. A hit, and Wingo could walk home.

The 2-0 pitch was a fastball down and maybe a touch away from Merrifield. The right-handed hitter, just as he was taught by his dad and his coaches, kept the barrel of the bat down as he extended. He hit a tough pitch with the sweet spot of the aluminum bat. The ball went out at a trajectory that could only be good. It would either be a sacrifice fly. Or it would drop.

It dropped.

Merrifield extended his arms and tongue as he ran to first base, knowing full well where the ball was headed and what was going on behind him. Wingo flung his helmet as he zipped down the baseline. He stomped on home plate, giving South Carolina a 2–1 victory—and the national championship.

Wingo's teammates came bounding onto the field before Wingo even got home. The Avatar Spirit Stick was closer to him than any Gamecock when he touched the plate.

But the victory transcended superstition. It transcended logic, in so many ways.

A team that did not win its division, much less its conference, had just captured the national championship. A team that did not have a first-, second- or third-round pick in the 2010 MLB draft had just won it all. A team that dropped four of five games entering the NCAA Tournament— one that had to rally to win every one of its Regional games, including the opener against lowly Bucknell—had snared the NCAA title. A team that had to win four consecutive games just to play on in Omaha did that against rather long odds.

A team that played for a one-of-a-kind friend had won for him. Merrifield found Rob Teal in the madness.

"I felt Bayler's hand on my bat," Merrifield told Teal.

UCLA
JUNE 29, 2010, ROSENBLATT STADIUM, OMAHA, NEBRASKA

SOUTH CAROLINA 2 (54-16)

Player	ab	r	h	rbi	bb	so	po	a	lob
Evan Marzilli lf	5	0	1	1	0	1	0	0	0
Whit Merrifield rf	5	0	1	1	0	1	0	0	0
Jackie Bradley Jr. cf	5	0	0	0	0	3	4	0	0
Christian Walker 1b	4	0	2	0	1	0	12	1	1
Adrian Morales 3b	5	0	0	0	0	2	0	4	4
Adam Matthews dh	3	0	0	0	0	0	0	0	0
Brady Thomas ph	1	0	1	0	0	0	0	0	0
Robert Beary pr	1	1	0	0	0	1	0	0	0
Kyle Enders c	3	0	1	0	2	0	8	0	0
Bobby Haney ss	5	0	2	0	0	1	3	3	1
Scott Wingo 2b	2	1	0	0	3	1	2	3	1
Michael Roth p	0	0	0	0	0	0	1	3	0
Jose Mata p	0	0	0	0	0	0	0	1	0
Tyler Webb p	0	0	0	0	0	0	0	0	0
John Taylor p	0	0	0	0	0	0	0	0	0
Matt Price p	0	0	0	0	0	0	0	0	0
Totals	39	2	8	2	6	10	30	15	7

UCLA 1 (51-17)

Player	ab	r	h	rbi	bb	so	po	a	lob
Niko Gallego ss	5	0	1	1	0	2	1	2	5
Beau Amaral cf	5	0	2	0	0	0	2	0	0
Blair Dunlap dh	4	0	1	0	0	0	0	0	0
Dean Espy 1b	3	0	0	0	1	1	11	0	1
Adrian Williams 2b	1	0	0	0	0	0	0	0	0
Cody Regis 2b/3b	5	0	0	0	0	2	2	2	3
Brett Krill rf	5	0	2	0	0	1	1	0	0
Chris Giovinazzo lf	3	0	0	0	1	0	1	0	0

Player	ab	r	h	rbi	bb	so	po	a	lob
Trevor Brown 3b/1b	4	1	2	0	0	1	2	2	0
Steve Rodriguez c	2	0	0	0	1	0	10	1	1
Rob Rasmussen p	0	0	0	0	0	0	0	3	0
Erik Goeddel p	0	0	0	0	0	0	0	0	0
Dan Klein p	0	0	0	0	0	0	1	2	0
Totals	**37**	**1**	**8**	**1**	**3**	**7**	**31**	**12**	**10**

Score by Innings				R H E	
UCLA	000	010	000	00 - 1 8 1	
South Carolina	000	000	010	01 - 2 9 1	

E—Espy (6); Morales (12). DP—SC 1. LOB—UCLA 10; SC 14. 2B: Amaral (12); Krill (14). HBP—Dunlap; Brown. SH—Giovinazzo (2); Rodriguez (10); Marzilli; Merrifield (15). CS—Gallego (2).

South Carolina	ip	h	r	er	bb	so	ab	bf	np
Michael Roth	5.0	6	1	1	2	3	17	20	78
Jose Mata	2.0	1	0	0	0	1	6	8	20
Tyler Webb	0.1	0	0	0	0	0	1	1	2
John Taylor	1.0	0	0	0	0	0	3	3	9
Matt Price	2.2	1	0	0	1	3	10	12	46

UCLA	ip	h	r	er	bb	so	ab	bf	np
Rob Rasmussen	6.0	6	0	0	4	5	23	28	109
Erik Goeddel	1.0	2	1	0	0	1	5	5	21
Dan Klein	3.1	1	1	1	2	4	11	14	75

Win—Price (5-1). Loss—Klein (6-1). Save—None.
WP—Klein (4). HBP—by Mata (Brown); by Price (Dunlap). PB—Rodriguez (7). Goeddel faced 1 batter in the 8th.

Umpires—HP: Gus Rodriguez; 1B: David Savage; 2B: Mark Ditsworth; 3B: A.J. Lostaglio
Start: 6:40 p.m.   Time: 4:15   Attendance: 24,390

Game notes
Game 2 of best-of-three championship series (South Carolina wins, 2-0).

RETURNING HEROES

JUNE 30, 2010

When Scott Wingo's right foot met home plate, officially signaling South Carolina's championship, the Gamecocks broke into a joyous and spontaneous celebration. So did Columbia. Simultaneously, Five Points was chaotic, with virtually the same scene unfolding in every bar and restaurant.

After the dog pile and trophy presentation, the Gamecocks continued the party at the team hotel. A small stage was set up, allowing for Ray Tanner and a few other players to speak to fans who had made the journey to Nebraska—including some who drove overnight to get there for the final two games. Football coach Steve Spurrier watched from the side of the room, grinning.

"Ray Tanner," Spurrier said, drawing out the syllables and nodding his head in approval.

Tanner took the stage a little after 1:00 a.m. He thanked the fans and then did something he said he would never do unless his team earned it. He thrust his index finger in the air.

South Carolina was No. 1.

"We're finally champions, first-time champions," said sophomore outfielder Jackie Bradley Jr., who was named the series' Most Outstanding Player after recording ten hits and driving in a CWS-high nine runs. "It's amazing. Not only did we make it here, we won it."

After fifty-four wins and sixteen losses, the Gamecocks were the only team in the country that could say it won its final game. No team before South Carolina had ever won six consecutive games in the College World Series.

There is no debate that pitching led the way. Paced by Blake Cooper, Matt Price and Michael Roth, Mark Calvi's staff allowed sixteen runs in sixty-eight innings in Omaha. It had a 2.11 ERA in those seven games. It gave up eight runs in the final five games. UCLA scored two runs in two games in the national championship series.

"That was our constant," Tanner said. "Pitching was the constant."

The Gamecocks turned off the College World Series lights at Rosenblatt Stadium in heart-racing, breathtaking fashion. They provided a thrill-a-minute experience to Omaha, as the city prepared to move the storied event to a new, state-of-the-art downtown ballpark.

Rosenblatt will never be forgotten. Neither will the 2010 College World Series—and its champion.

"I love the fact that we're here in the final chapter of Rosenblatt," Tanner said the day before the eight-team tournament began. "I feel like that's very special and unique. The history for the College World Series, for many years to come, will be Rosenblatt. Although the new doors will open next year, the history will be here."

The Gamecocks landed in Columbia the next day and immediately bused to Colonial Life Arena on campus. Whit Merrifield, author of the walk-off hit, suspected a few thousand would meet them inside the arena. The team walked inside to find fifteen thousand fans—more than the regular attendance for a basketball game—awaiting their arrival. They roared when the Gamecocks appeared to the theme from *2001: A Space Odyssey*.

"You first have to dream it before you see it," Tanner said, voice rising as he addressed the crowd. "I've dreamed it, and now I see it."

The celebration in Columbia began again, and this time the team was around to enjoy it. Captains Kyle Enders and Jay Brown led the procession, holding the championship trophy above their heads. Queen's "We Are the Champions" played as the Gamecocks made their way around the arena floor, displaying the trophy and high-fiving as many people as they could.

A line in the song about "fighting to the end" is typically so cliché with championship teams. But South Carolina, down to its final strike in Omaha, had done that. So had some important people who did not live to see the Gamecocks win it all. Tanner dedicated the title to three people. One was

Sarge Frye, who worked in the athletic department for forty-five years. Frye, who died in 2002, had the old baseball stadium named for him in 1980. The second was Tom Price, the school's longtime sports information director who was the color man on the team's radio broadcasts. He died in 2008. The new stadium's press box is named for him.

The third was Bayler Teal, the seven-year-old who had been adopted in 2008 by the team and died during the College World Series. In the crowd, doctors and nurses from Palmetto Health Children's Hospital wore T-shirts with Bayler's name on them and held up "Baylerball" signs. They were grieving the loss while celebrating the Gamecocks' win.

"A national championship would mean a great deal, no matter what," Roth said. "But, given the circumstances, it also means that much more. When I look back on it, ten years later, I'm not just going to remember that I threw a nine-inning game in Omaha in my first start of the year. I'm going to remember the feelings of Bayler passing away and meeting his father. I'll remember winning the whole thing, but I'll also remember his family coming out there and us paying tribute to Bayler and his family just after receiving the national championship trophy."

Bayler's legacy lives on. After returning home, the Teals started a fund, Bayler's Prayers, to help families cope with pediatric cancer. Rob, who didn't work so he could spend time with Bayler, received a sales job soon after getting back from Omaha. A company had seen the family's story on TV. Bridges has found his own sport: basketball. He's the only player on his team who can dribble. He swears he will be able to dunk by his seventh birthday. He misses his brother and best friend but tells everyone that Bayler is in Heaven. He's enjoying having the spotlight all to himself, but that will not last long.

Risha is expecting a baby girl this summer.

The day after the reception at the arena, Tanner received from Governor Mark Sanford the Order of the Palmetto, the highest civilian honor in the state of South Carolina. The day after that, Tanner and the Gamecocks rode down Main Street in a ticker-tape parade that ended at the State House steps. Above the capitol building, the University of South Carolina flag was raised to join the American and state flags. It was the first time that it had ever flown atop the State House.

New Columbia mayor Steve Benjamin, in his first official act, awarded Tanner the key to the city. More than forty thousand people, some leaning out high-rise windows, lined the downtown streets and crowded in front of the State House to pay tribute to the Gamecocks.

"I always like to give credit to our players between the lines," Tanner told the crowd, "but without you, outside the lines, this was not possible."

Then, just as he had done in the team hotel and arena, second baseman Scott Wingo led the fans in the barking-dog breakdown.

In September, the Gamecocks were one of thirty title-winning teams to meet President Barack Obama at the White House.

Tanner has been asked several times where the 2010 team would rank, in terms of talent, among those he's coached at South Carolina.

"Seventh?" Tanner says. "Maybe eighth?"

South Carolina did not have the best players in the NCAA Tournament. But it had the best team.

It would have been something special if the school won a national championship in any major sport and in any conceivable way. But the 2010 Gamecocks baseball team will be a tough story to top.

"You don't want to say it was a once-in-a-lifetime thing, but that was a once-in-a-lifetime thing," Holbrook said. "Can we win another one? Sure. But it won't be like that. There's no way."

AUTHOR'S NOTE

DECEMBER 24, 2008

When I walked into the Hardee's in Bishopville on Christmas Eve in 2008, I could not have known how my life was about to dramatically change. I drove the forty-five minutes from Columbia to meet with Rob and Risha Teal, whose son Bayler had been diagnosed with cancer two months earlier. I was told that South Carolina's baseball team had adopted the family that Christmas. I thought it was a generous gesture, and I wanted to do a holiday story on the family.

Honestly, I never thought I would see the Teals again after that morning. I was hopeful, though, that Bayler would beat cancer and normalcy would return for the family.

I did see the Teals again. It was twenty months later in a hotel in Omaha, Nebraska. It was about an hour after the Gamecocks had won the national title. We hugged and smiled. Outwardly, I was thrilled for them. Inside, I hurt for them. What unfathomable heartache and pain they had endured since I had last seen them.

Journalists are taught to keep professional distance, but exceptions must be made, and I'm unafraid to walk into the gray area when circumstances are as powerful as a little boy dying of cancer and a team improbably winning a championship in his honor. Rob and Risha are two of the most personable, genuine people I know. I was drawn to them, just as so many of their friends have been. The personalities on South Carolina's baseball team were likewise magnetic.

My heart was crushed when I learned, in the ninth inning of the second Oklahoma game, that Bayler had died. I had just talked to Rob the day before, because I planned to write an update story for that Friday's paper. About 10:00 p.m. that Thursday night, an editor called to ask if I had heard anything about Bayler dying. I said I had not and the only person I could ask, besides Rob, was Chad Holbrook—and he was in the third-base coaching box at the time. I didn't want to, but I called Rob's cellphone. Rob's mom answered. She was crying. She told me Bayler had died a few minutes earlier.

Stunned, I walked back to my seat in the press box and tried my best to conceal the fact that I was a disaster inside. Independent of Bayler, it was a very important game. It could have been the end of the season for the Gamecocks. But, as you know, the game was not at all independent of Bayler. On deadline, I had to start writing something when South Carolina fell behind 2–1 in the top of the twelfth inning.

The draft I wrote was about the fact that you lose in life sometimes. South Carolina had lost a baseball game. Bayler had lost his life. But that story never ran. Thank God it never ran. I deleted it a few minutes later because Bayler had taught the Gamecocks something about fighting. I held back tears as I watched Jackie Bradley Jr., down to the season's final strike, tie the game with a hit and then come around to score the winning run.

Given the context, and my own unlikely personal involvement, it was the most defining moment I have ever personally seen in sports. I doubt I will ever see anything to top it. It's timing that I will never, ever comprehend.

Bayler met the Gamecocks in October 2008 and saw them several times after that, even throwing out a first pitch in March 2010. How could he possibly die in the middle of one of the program and College World Series' most dramatic games of all time? Was his divine aid required?

What an intricate design Bayler's life had, right down to his final day, hour and minute. There was beautiful poetry written, even in that unjust death. I am not wise enough to know or understand whether bigger powers are at play in our lives, but I have never seen a more compelling argument that God is real, He does play a part in our lives and He does love us— even through the worst of times. He is a God of Romans 8:28, which says He causes all things to work together for good. All things. I believed that before Bayler, but my faith in that verse has grown exponentially since those fourteen days in Omaha. Without Jesus, I would be nothing. Because of him I live—and live an abundant life. Omaha was as abundant as life gets. I'm sure the Gamecocks agree with me.

December 24, 2008

Thank you to my family, and particularly my parents, for encouragement and support in literally everything I have ever done. Thank you for the sacrifices you made for me to be where I am today. Those things never went unnoticed.

Thanks to my wonderful circle of friends, including some fantastic pro bono copy editors—Dan, Gene, Kristin and Michael. Your eyes and ideas were vital in taking my limited vision and casting it wider. Got to give a special thank-you to my best friend, Drew, who was so instrumental that he can take credit for coming up with the title. The draft was rough until it met Drew. I got you on your first book, buddy. Thanks, also, to Kent for helping me hatch this idea in Kansas City the day after the College World Series. We sketched an outline on bar napkins. Got to start somewhere, right?

Thanks so much to The History Press for believing in me and this project. That means the world to a first-time author. You gave me the easel and canvas and stepped away, allowing me to splash the color as I saw fit. I hope the picture is pleasing. Thanks, too, to Kyle and Rob for referring me to The History Press. Without you guys, I might still be seeking a publisher. Thanks, also, to Chris for helping set up a website for the book. I know nothing about page design; I have never been more aware of that fact.

Thanks to those at South Carolina—the players, coaches and staff members—who were so generous with their time. I needed your stories. I needed your voices. Without your candor, this book would have been lifeless. With you, it has a personality. Thanks, in particular, to Ray Tanner, Chad Holbrook, Mark Calvi and Sammy Esposito. You let me camp out at Carolina Stadium, and I appreciate it. Thanks to one of the nicest guys I know, sports information whiz Andrew Kitick, for your patience with me. I had request after request for you, and you responded with such grace each time. You're a true gentleman.

Of course, I owe a great deal of gratitude to Rob and Risha for opening up their lives to me. I'm grateful to count you as good friends, even if it hurts to know it is as a result of tragedy. Your strength and faith are inspiring to me every day of my life. I thank Bayler, too, for living seven and a half big, brave and bold years. Your legacy will outshine most everyone I know. I look forward to meeting you one day. I am glad to know you are not in pain anymore.

I hope there is baseball in Heaven.

				CHAMPIONSH

FLORIDA STATE 1

TCU 3

TCU 8

GAME 6

GAME 1

UCLA 2

BRACKET 1

UCLA

UCLA 11

UCLA 6

UCLA 10

South Carolin

FLORIDA 3

GAME 11

GAME 13

GAME 1

GAME 2

UCLA

TCU 11

TCU 3

TCU 6

South Carolina

FLORIDA STATE 8

FLORIDA STATE 7

GAME 2

FLORIDA 5

GAME 9

GAME 5

WORLD SERIES BRACKET ❖

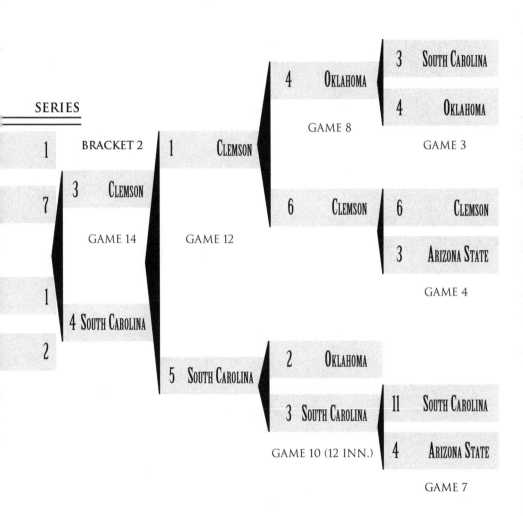

SERIES

BRACKET 2

1		1	CLEMSON	4	OKLAHOMA	3 SOUTH CAROLINA
						4 OKLAHOMA
7	3 CLEMSON					GAME 3
				GAME 8		
	GAME 14	GAME 12				
				6	CLEMSON	6 CLEMSON
1						3 ARIZONA STATE
	4 SOUTH CAROLINA					GAME 4
2		5	SOUTH CAROLINA	2	OKLAHOMA	
						11 SOUTH CAROLINA
				3	SOUTH CAROLINA	4 ARIZONA STATE
				GAME 10 (12 INN.)		GAME 7

2010 SOUTH CAROLINA GAMECOCKS BASEBALL STATS

GAMES RESULTS

* = Conference game
! = SEC Tournament (Hoover, Ala.)
@ = NCAA Regional (Columbia, S.C.)
() extra inning game

Date	Opponent	Score	I	Overall	SEC	Pitcher of record	Att.	Time
02/19	DUQUESNE	W 10–3	9	1-0-0	0-0-0	Cooper (W 1-0)	6,380	2:28
02/20	DUQUESNE	W 13–3	9	2-0-0	0-0-0	Dyson (W 1-0)	7,926	3:08
02/21	DUQUESNE	W 5–3	9	3-0-0	0-0-0	Neff (W 1-0)	6,910	2:11
02/26	at #13 East Carolina	W 6–2	9	4-0-0	0-0-0	Cooper (W 2-0)	3,214	3:07
02/27	at #13 East Carolina	L 3–4	9	4-1-0	0-0-0	Taylor (L 0-1)	4,461	2:59
02/28	at #13 East Carolina	L 2–4	9	4-2-0	0-0-0	Neff (L 1-1)	3,743	2:21
03/03	PRESBYTERIAN	W 15–0	9	5-2-0	0-0-0	Belcher (W 1-0)	5,217	2:43
03/05	at #9 Clemson	L 3–4	9	5-3-0	0-0-0	Roth (L 0-1)	6,346	2:28
03/06	vs #9 Clemson	W 7–5	9	6-3-0	0-0-0	Price (W 1-0)	7,105	3:15
03/07	#9 CLEMSON	L 6–19	9	6-4-0	0-0-0	Webb (L 0-1)	8,214	3:23
03/09	VALPARAISO	W 12–4	9	7-4-0	0-0-0	Mata (W 1-0)	5,295	2:32
03/10	VALPARAISO	W 7–3	9	8-4-0	0-0-0	Price (W 2-0)	4,902	2:25
03/13	BROWN-1	W 8–4	9	9-4-0	0-0-0	Cooper (W 3-0)	5,053	2:24
03/13	BROWN-2	W 10–7	9	10-4-0	0-0-0	Brown (W 1-0)	5,250	2:44
03/14	BROWN	W 6–5	(10)	11-4-0	0-0-0	Revan (W 1-0)	5,307	3:17
03/16	at Furman	W 15–0	9	12-4-0	0-0-0	Belcher (W 2-0)	3,256	2:37

Date	Opponent	Score	I	Overall	SEC	Pitcher of record	Att.	Time
03/17	DAVIDSON	W 8–3	9	13-4-0	0-0-0	Mata (W 2-0)	5,054	2:53
*03/19	TENNESSEE	W 4–2	9	14-4-0	1-0-0	Carter (W 1-0)	6,211	2:37
*03/20	TENNESSEE	W 10–7	9	15-4-0	2-0-0	Bangs (W 1-0)	7,813	2:53
*03/21	TENNESSEE	W 4–0	9	16-4-0	3-0-0	Webb (W 1-1)	5,629	2:30
03/23	at Georgia Southern	W 8–5	(13)	17-4-0	3-0-0	Taylor (W 1-1)	2,022	4:45
*03/26	at Auburn	W 11–5	9	18-4-0	4-0-0	Cooper (W 4-0)	3,458	2:55
*03/27	at Auburn	W 2–0	9	19-4-0	5-0-0	Dyson (W 2-0)	2,970	2:26
*03/28	at Auburn	L 6–10	9	19-5-0	5-1-0	Webb (L 1-2)	2,316	2:52
03/30	#25 THE CITADEL	W 10–1	9	20-5-0	5-1-0	Holmes (W 1-0)	6,451	2:36
*04/02	MISSISSIPPI STATE	W 10–2	9	21-5-0	6-1-0	Cooper (W 5-0)	7,019	2:32
*04/03	MISSISSIPPI STATE	L 7–8	9	21-6-0	6-2-0	Dyson (L 2-1)	7,012	3:49
*04/04	MISSISSIPPI STATE	W 14–2	9	22-6-0	7-2-0	Price (W 3-0)	5,576	3:04
04/07	COLL. OF CHARLESTON	W 6–3	9	23-6-0	7-2-0	Holmes (W 2-0)	7,523	2:50
04/09	at #19 Vanderbilt	W 3–2	9	24-6-0	8-2-0	Cooper (W 6-0)	2,853	2:23
*04/10	at #19 Vanderbilt	L 2–8	9	24-7-0	8-3-0	Dyson (L 2-2)	3,197	2:31
*04/11	at #19 Vanderbilt	W 2–0	9	25-7-0	9-3-0	Brown (W 2-0)	2,328	2:14
04/14	at The Citadel	W 10–4	9	26-7-0	9-3-0	Taylor (W 2-1)	4,087	2:51
*04/16	#14 OLE MISS	W 5–0	9	27-7-0	10-3-0	Cooper (W 7-0)	7,094	2:45
*04/17	#14 OLE MISS	W 9–5	9	28-7-0	11-3-0	Dyson (W 3-2)	7,952	2:48
*04/18	#14 OLE MISS	L 4–5	9	28-8-0	11-4-0	Taylor (L 2-2)	7,585	2:54
04/20	USC UPSTATE	W 4–2	9	29-8-0	11-4-0	Mata (W 3-0)	6,409	2:27
*04/23	at Georgia	W 11-4	9	30-8-0	12-4-0	Cooper (W 8-0)	2,642	2:41
*04/25	at Georgia-1	W 5–0	7	31-8-0	13-4-0	Dyson (W 4-2)		2:06
*04/25	at Georgia-2	W 8–7	7	32-8-0	14-4-0	Carter (W 2-0)	3,169	2:49
*04/30	ALABAMA	W 9–7	(11)	33-8-0	15-4-0	Mata (W 4-0)	8,145	3:43
*05/01	ALABAMA	L 4–6	9	33-9-0	15-5-0	Dyson (L 4-3)	8,053	2:41
*05/02	ALABAMA	W 20–15	9	34-9-0	16-5-0	Webb (W 2-2)	8,006	3:23
05/05	WINTHROP	W 14–6	9	35-9-0	16-5-0	Mata (W 5-0)	6,014	2:58
*05/07	at Kentucky	W 13–9	9	36-9-0	17-5-0	Cooper (W 9-0)	2,183	3:34

2010 SOUTH CAROLINA GAMECOCKS BASEBALL STATS

Date	Opponent	Score	I	Overall	SEC	Pitcher of record	Att.	Time
*05/08	at Kentucky	L 1–2	9	36-10-0	17-6-0	Dyson (L 4-4)	1,755	2:31
*05/09	at Kentucky	L 3–9	9	36-11-0	17-7-0	Mata (L 5-1)	1,702	3:04
05/11	WOFFORD	W 17–4	9	37-11-0	17-7-0	Belcher (W 3-0)	6,402	2:59
05/12	CHARLESTON SOUTHERN	W 10–2	9	38-11-0	17-7-0	Mata (W 6-1)	6,573	2:45
*05/14	at #10 Arkansas	W 3–2	9	39-11-0	18-7-0	Cooper (W 10-0)	9,622	2:34
*05/15	at #10 Arkansas	W 5–0	9	40-11-0	19-7-0	Dyson (W 5-4)	8,670	2:08
*05/16	at #10 Arkansas	W 5–3	9	41-11-0	20-7-0	Taylor (W 3-2)	8,227	2:50
05/18	FURMAN	W 11–6	9	42-11-0	20-7-0	Neff (W 2-1)	6,291	2:56
*05/20	#4 FLORIDA	L 2–3	9	42-12-0	20-8-0	Cooper (L 10-1)	8,188	3:01
*05/21	#4 FLORIDA	L 2–5	9	42-13-0	20-9-0	Dyson (L 5-5)	8,242	3:07
*05/22	#4 FLORIDA	W 11–6	9	43-13-0	21-9-0	Brown (W 3-0)	7,523	3:01
!05/26	vs #21 Ole Miss	L 0–3	9	43-14-0	21-9-0	Belcher (L 3-1)	12,514	2:39
!05/27	vs #13 Auburn	L 1–3	(12)	43-15-0	21-9-0	Price (L 3-1)	5,759	3:12
@06/04	BUCKNELL	W 9–5	9	44-15-0	21-9-0	Roth (W 1-1)	6,712	2:58
@06/05	THE CITADEL	W 9–4	9	45-15-0	21-9-0	Cooper (W 11-1)	7,418	2:45
@06/06	VIRGINIA TECH	W 10–2	9	46-15-0	21-9-0	Mata (W 7-1)	6,233	2:41
#06/12	at Coastal Carolina	W 4–3	9	47-15-0	21-9-0	Cooper (W 12-1)	6,599	3:31
#06/13	at Coastal Carolina	W 10–9	9	48-15-0	21-9-0	Carter (W 3-0)	6,599	3:46
$06/20	vs Oklahoma	L 3–4	9	48-16-0	21-9-0	Cooper (L 12-2)	22,835	2:53
$06/22	vs Arizona State	W 11–4	9	49-16-0	21-9-0	Dyson (W 6-5)	19,936	3:09
$06/24	vs Oklahoma	W 3–2	(12)	50-16-0	21-9-0	Webb (W 3-2)	24,180	3:46
$06/25	vs Clemson	W 5–1	9	51-16-0	21-9-0	Roth (W 2-1)	22,194	2:22
$06/26	vs Clemson	W 4–3	9	52-16-0	21-9-0	Price (W 4-1)	12,593	3:04
$06/28	vs UCLA	W 7–1	9	53-16-0	21-9-0	Cooper (W 13-2)	23,181	3:28
$06/29	vs UCLA	W 2–1	(11)	54-16-0	21-9-0	Price (W 5-1)	24,390	4:15

GAMES SUMMARY

(All games)

Score by innings	1	2	3	4	5	6	7	8	9	Extra	Total
South Carolina	55	70	77	56	43	52	60	60	17	9	499
Opponents	34	40	33	37	23	22	35	30	28	3	285

Record when...

Overall	**54-16**
Conference	21-9
Non-Conference	33-7
Home games	30-6
Away games	17-7
Neutral site	7-3
Day games	25-12
Night games	29-4
vs Left starter	20-7
vs Right starter	34-9
1-Run games	9-7
2-Run games	8-3
5+-Run games	25-3
Extra innings	5-1
Shutouts	8-1

Scoring

0–2 runs	3-7
3–5 runs	14-6
6–9 runs	14-3
10+ runs	23-0

Opponent

0–2 runs	22-1
3–5 runs	22-9
6–9 runs	9-4
10+ runs	1-2
Scored in 1st inning	26-2
Opp. scored in 1st	15-6
Scores first	36-6
Opp. scores first	18-10

After 6		After 7		After 8	
Leading	41-1	Leading	42-1	Leading	49-1
Trailing	6-12	Trailing	5-13	Trailing	0-14
Tied	7-3	Tied	5-2	Tied	3-1

Hit 0 home runs	14-7	Made 0 errors	21-5
1 home run	15-7	1 error	20-9
2+ home runs	25-2	2+ errors	13-2
Opponent 0 home runs	24-7	Opp. made 0 errors	14-7
1 home run	22-4	1 error	16-6
2+ HRs	8-5	2+ errors	24-3

Out-hit opponent	45-5
Out-hit by opponent	4-8
Hits are tied	5-3

2010 South Carolina Gamecocks Baseball Stats

Record when team scores:

Runs	0	1	2	3	4	5	6	7	8	9	10+
W-L	0-1	0-2	3-4	3-4	5-2	6-0	3-2	3-1	4-0	4-0	23-0

Record when opponent scores:

Runs	0	1	2	3	4	5	6	7	8	9	10+
W-L	8-0	4-0	10-1	9-3	7-4	6-2	3-1	4-0	0-2	2-1	1-2

Record when leading after:

Inning	1	2	3	4	5	6	7	8
W-L	24-2	34-2	36-3	38-2	38-1	41-1	42-1	49-1

Record when trailing after:

Inning	1	2	3	4	5	6	7	8
W-L	9-5	9-8	7-9	9-10	8-12	6-12	5-13	0-14

Record when tied after:

Inning	1	2	3	4	5	6	7	8
W-L	21-9	11-6	11-4	7-4	8-3	7-3	5-2	3-1

Current winning streak: 6
Longest winning streak: 13
Longest losing streak: 2

Home attendance: 241,582 (36 dates avg = 6,710)
Away attendance: 270,106 (33 dates avg = 8,185)
Total attendance: 511,688 (69 dates avg = 7,415)

SEASON BOX SCORE

Record: 54-16   Home: 30-6   Away: 17-7   Neutral: 7-3   SEC: 21-9

Player	avg	gp-gs	ab	r	h	2b	3b	hr	rbi	tb
19 Jackie Bradley Jr.	.368	67-61	242	56	89	12	1	13	60	142
36 Brady Thomas	.331	47-33	139	37	46	13	1	8	30	85
13 Christian Walker	.327	61-51	226	35	74	12	2	9	51	117
5 Whit Merrifield	.321	70-70	296	72	95	12	1	13	42	148
26 Adam Matthews	.307	64-56	189	30	58	12	2	7	31	95
18 Kyle Enders	.281	61-51	185	26	52	9	1	3	32	72
3 Adrian Morales	.273	68-59	245	50	67	15	0	9	56	109
47 Nick Ebert	.272	45-32	125	27	34	7	1	7	31	64
23 Bobby Haney	.263	64-61	217	30	57	8	1	3	24	76
8 Scott Wingo	.247	70-66	198	52	49	8	3	9	31	90
-------------										
31 Evan Marzilli	.385	63-19	91	30	35	8	0	3	12	52
7 Richard Royal	.333	2-0	3	1	1	0	0	0	1	1
6 Jeffery Jones	.300	47-30	110	21	33	7	0	8	29	64
4 Robert Beary	.276	44-22	98	18	27	3	1	1	14	35
42 Parker Bangs	.267	28-17	60	10	16	6	0	3	18	31
29 Michael Roth	.111	9-19	2	1	0	0	1	1	4	.444
24 Brison Celek	.000	9-18	2	0	0	0	0	0	0	.000
16 Austin Ashmore	.000	5-0	3	0	0	0	0	0	0	0
9 Steven Neff	.000	1-0	0	0	0	0	0	0	0	0
Totals	**.300**	**70**	**2444**	**499**	**734**	**132**	**14**	**97**	**463**	**1185**
Opponents	.226	70	2329	285	527	70	6	61	258	792

LOB—Team (586), Opp (496). DPs turned—Team (62), Opp (57). CI—Team (1), Thomas 1, Opp (1). IBB—Team (9), Bradley 2, Jones 2, Ebert 2, Merrifield 1, Matthews 1, Morales 1, Opp (6). Picked off—Morales 2, Merrifield 2, Bradley 2, Enders 2, Wingo 1, Walker 1, Ebert 1.

slg%	bb	hp	so	gdp	ob%	sf	sh	sb-att	po	a	e	fld%
.587	41	8	37	4	.473	1	1	7-10	147	5	1	.993
.612	14	2	33	5	.400	0	1	3-5	185	11	3	.985
.518	18	4	18	9	.384	2	2	2-3	353	30	9	.977
.500	3v0	6	36	4	.393	1	15	12-18	85	28	5	.958
.503	25	2	42	1	.392	1	5	7-9	56	0	3	.949
.389	21	7	35	3	.370	3	6	2-4	438	33	4	.992
.445	18	13	32	8	.348	6	9	5-9	52	131	12	.938
.512	26	7	30	3	.416	3	1	0-0	191	13	2	.990
.350	14	2	38	1	.309	3	3	1-1	83	162	6	.976
.455	37	18	48	2	.409	1	9	2-3	116	200	12	.963
.571	17	8	20	0	.513	1	2	8-8	41	0	3	.932
.333	0	0	2	0	.333	0	0	0-0	1	0	0	1.000
.582	22	3	14	0	.423	2	1	0-0	81	3	0	1.000
.357	4	6	21	2	.339	1	3	3-4	32	1	0	1.000
.517	9	1	19	0	.366	1	0	1-1	0	0	0	.000
1	0	3	0	.200	0	0	0-0	9	11	0	1.000	
1	2	4	2	.273	0	0	0-0	0	0	0	.000	
.000	0	0	2	0	.000	0	0	0-0	0	0	0	.000
.000	0	0	0	0	.000	0	0	0-0	1	3	1	.800
.485	298	89	434	44	.392	26	58	53-75	1901	726	66	.975
.340	220	74	625	53	.311	15	43	43-66	1831	712	99	.963

2010 South Carolina Gamecocks Baseball Stats

Player	era	w-l	app	gs	cg	sho	sv	ip	h
27 Blake Cooper	2.76	13-2	20	20	1	1/0	0	137.0	111
20 Sam Dyson	4.28	6-5	18	18	3	2/1	0	103.0	98
--------------------									
34 Jordan Propst	0.00	0-0	2	0	0	0/1	0	1.0	1
29 Michael Roth	1.34	2-1	37	2	1	0/3	3	40.1	27
39 Patrick Sullivan	1.50	0-0	7	0	0	0/1	0	6.0	7
22 Matt Price	2.26	5-1	31	0	0	0/4	10	55.2	37
17 Jose Mata	2.40	7-1	33	0	0	0/0	0	45.0	35
15 Nolan Belcher	2.43	3-1	11	6	0	0/2	0	29.2	18
14 John Taylor	3.38	3-2	28	0	0	0/1	1	29.1	27
38 Tyler Webb	3.96	3-2	17	7	0	0/1	0	36.1	29
9 Steven Neff	4.11	2-1	17	1	0	0/0	0	15.1	16
37 Jay Brown	4.44	3-0	17	9	0	0/2	0	50.2	46
12 Jimmy Revan	4.85	1-0	9	1	0	0/0	0	13.0	8
42 Parker Bangs	5.27	1-0	14	0	0	0/1	0	13.2	7
44 Colby Holmes	5.33	2-0	11	6	0	0/1	0	27.0	29
32 Ethan Carter	5.46	3-0	24	0	0	0/1	2	28.0	25
33 Alex Burrell	13.50	0-0	2	0	0	0/0	0	2.2	6
Totals	**3.45**	**54-16**	**70**	**70**	**5**	**8/5**	**16**	**633.2**	**527**
Opponents	6.16	16-54	70	70	1	1/	9	610.1	734

PB—Team (13), Enders 11, Thomas 2, Opp (14). Pickoffs—Team (5), Roth 3, Thomas 1, Mata 1, Opp (10). SBA/ATT—Enders (21-38), Thomas (22-25), Cooper (5-14), Dyson (9-10), Belcher (7-8), Price (3-6), Mata (2-5), Roth (2-5), Brown (2-3), Webb (2-3), Neff (2-3), Bangs (3-3), Holmes (2-2), Sullivan (2-2), Taylor (1-1), Carter (1-1).

2010 South Carolina Gamecocks Baseball Stats

r	er	bb	so	2b	3b	hr	b/avg	wp	hp	bk	sfa	sha
52	42	39	126	13	0	12	.223	1	15	0	3	6
55	49	24	101	14	2	6	.249	5	20	1	5	9
0	0	0	2	0	0	0	.250	0	1	0	0	0
8	6	10	35	3	0	1	.196	0	4	0	0	3
4	1	4	7	1	0	1	.292	2	0	1	1	0
16	14	19	83	4	1	4	.183	0	9	0	0	0
15	12	10	37	5	1	2	.215	1	3	0	1	3
10	8	18	32	1	0	2	.184	5	2	0	1	4
14	11	5	17	3	0	3.24	3	0	3	0	1	2
17	16	13	36	3	0	6	.218	0	4	0	1	1
8	7	8	16	3	0	1	.276	1	3	2	0	2
30	25	21	34	7	0	10	.246	1	3	1	0	8
8	7	13	20	2	0	2	.167	1	1	0	0	0
8	8	9	21	1	1	2	.146	1	2	0	0	0
18	16	16	27	3	0	6	.266	2	2	2	1	1
18	17	9	30	7	1	3	.245	0	2	0	1	4
4	4	2	1	0	0	0	.462	0	0	0	0	0
285	**243**	**220**	**625**	**70**	**6**	**61**	**.226**	**20**	**74**	**7**	**15**	**43**
499	418	298	434	132	14	97	.300	61	89	6	2	58

TWITTER TIMELINE

@gamecocksblog
June 24–30, 2010

The Gamecocks HAVE to win tonight, right? How could SC and Clemson be here and the teams not play? Wouldn't seem right.
Thursday, June 24, 6:50 p.m.

RT @Mark_HaseldenMN Sean McDonough just explained the Avatar Spirit Stick to ESPN2 viewers.
Thursday, June 24, 8:13 p.m.

Michael Roth coming in now to face Reine. Cooper is done after 5 2/3 IP, 98 pitches. Tip your cap. Wow. Great outing on three days' rest.
Thursday, June 24, 8:44 p.m.

Just heard a national baseball writer said Cooper was just OK. You've got to be kidding me. What game are you watching?
Thursday, June 24, 8:47 p.m.

Jackie Bradley is 0-3 tonight after that first-pitch groundout. That, friends, might be when you panic if you're an SC fan.
Thursday, June 24, 8:53 p.m.

Ya look up at the scoreboard all of a sudden, and it's 1–0 in the 8th. Wow.
Well-played game so far. SC short on time.
Thursday, June 24, 9:15 p.m.

Christian Walker doesn't just hit 3-run homers. He singles through left side
and it's a 1–1 game. BIG hit for frosh, scoring another frosh.
Thursday, June 24, 9:33 p.m.

I'll say it again: This is a GREAT baseball game. Probably the best I've seen
this year, or in long time.
Thursday, June 24, 9:49 p.m.

Just to completely humble me and all going on, just learned 7-year-old Bayler
Teal—a HUGE Gamecock fan—just succumbed to cancer.
Thursday, June 24, 10:11 p.m.

The Gamecocks have dedicated this College World Series to him. I actually
had an A1 story on him ready to run tomorrow. It'll wait a day.
Thursday, June 24, 10:12 p.m.

@Cocky2001 tells me the team knows about Bayler's passing. Don't they
HAVE to win this one? Who's it going to be?
Thursday, June 24, 10:14 p.m.

Carter's second pitch is hammered into right-center-field seats by Ogle, who
is taking over for Bradley as CWS' hottest hitter. 2-1 OU.
Thursday, June 24, 10:30 p.m.

Beary-Marzilli-Merrifield are last hacks for Gamecocks. Vs. OU closer Ryan
Duke.
Thursday, June 24, 10:40 p.m.

Robert Beary, after two miserable ABs, comes thru with leadoff single. RISP,
anyone?
Thursday, June 24, 10:42 p.m.

Season down to SC's best hitters, Merrifield and Bradley.
Thursday, June 24, 10:46 p.m.

Beary steals second without a throw. Getting tense.
Thursday, June 24, 10:47 p.m.

Merrifield pops up in foul territory. 2 down. Bradley up in HUGE spot. Here's your season, folks.
Thursday, June 24, 10:48 p.m.

Gamecocks down to final strike. 2-2 count to Bradley. Tying run on second.
Thursday, June 24, 10:50 p.m.

Jackie Bradley.
Thursday, June 24, 10:51 p.m.

Bradley singles thru right side. Beary scores from second. Tied again 2–2. What a game!
Thursday, June 24, 10:51 p.m.

That's IT! Gamecocks win. Brady Thomas with single up middle. BALLGAME. 3–2 Gamecocks win. Amazing.
Thursday, June 24, 10:56 p.m.

I'm not Gamecock fan, at all, but I'm tearing up right now. That one was for Bayler. No doubt in my mind. He's in Heaven. So are Gamecocks.
Thursday, June 24, 10:57 p.m.

What a day. Went from poop floating around my hotel room to one of best games I've ever witnessed in my life.
Friday, June 25, 12:16 a.m.

Michael Roth is your starter tonight for Gamecocks. He went an inning and a third last night. It's a Johnny Wholestaff night. SC HAS to hit.
Friday, June 25, 12:35 p.m.

Roth with a 1-2-3 6th inning. Wow. Who saw him going this long? Ha, I said he'd pitch first 2 innings. He's been outstanding.
Friday, June 25, 10:50 p.m.

Roth has a 1-2-3 7th inning—all groundballs. Whoa. That's 15 ground-ball outs in game. That was a SEVEN-pitch seventh inning. 77 pitches.
Friday, June 25, 11:02 p.m.

They just announced this is Roth's longest outing of his career. Uh, yeah...a while ago. It was 4 1/3 IP last year vs CofC.
Friday, June 25, 11:12 p.m.

RT @jboxt1 Tell you what; a lot of people/doubters owe Mark Calvi an FTP fruit basket or something.
Friday, June 25, 11:27 p.m.

Roth strikes out Hinson to end the game. What a stirring performance for the reliever, a LH specialist. A three-hit complete game. 5–1 SC.
Friday, June 25, 11:35 p.m.

Final: South Carolina 5, Clemson 1. Let's do it again tomorrow.
Friday, June 25, 11:35 p.m.

I thought I'd be covering a game here tomorrow night. NEVER thought it would be because of Michael Roth's CG 3-hitter.
Saturday, June 26, 12:52 a.m.

RT @cholbrook2: Bayler is watching over us!
Saturday, June 26, 1:01 a.m.

Drunk Clemson fans, upon my return to the hotel: "At least we don't have to see Roth tomorrow."
Saturday, June 26, 3:18 a.m.

Final: South Carolina 4, Clemson 3. Gamecocks two wins from national title. Dyson was great on 3 days' rest, team found way.
Saturday, June 26, 11:02 p.m.

Great seasons for both Clemson and South Carolina. Really, really great. Gamecocks just happen to be moving on.
Saturday, June 26, 11:32 p.m.

Getting ready to head out to national championship news conference, for UCLA and South Carolina. Who thought we'd be saying that?
Sunday, June 27, 11:10 p.m.

From the only-in-SC file. RT @TreyWalker: Gamecocks victory over Tigers gets worked into sermon from pulpit today
Sunday, June 27, 12:27 p.m.

Have any of you guys stopped today and thought, "Wait, South Carolina is playing for a national championship?"
Sunday, June 27, 6:09 p.m.

RT @cholbrook2: Win, lose, or draw I'm proud!
Sunday, June 27, 6:30 p.m.

I'm sitting alone in the Rosenblatt press box. Giving me chills.
Sunday, June 27, 6:43 p.m.

OK, listen up friends. Here's chance to help Teal family after their loss this wk. Rob, Risha and 5-yr-old Bridges actually coming to Omaha.
Sunday, June 27, 7:18 p.m.

The Teals, who just had funeral for 7-yr-old Bayler, are expected to be here tomorrow for the first pitch between Gamecocks and Bruins.
Sunday, June 27, 7:18 p.m.

I just posted on my blog a way to donate to a fund that would pay for their trip here to Omaha.
Sunday, June 27, 7:19 p.m.

We should do this, to show them our hearts in a time of great sorrow. We should allow them to enjoy it as the Gamecocks play for Bayler.
Sunday, June 27, 7:19 p.m.

My money is where my mouth is. As soon as I get home, I'm donating $100 to Bayler's fund, to help them pay for the trip.
Sunday, June 27, 7:20 p.m.

UCLA hijinx? South Carolina team hotel fire alarms going off at 1:30 am. Swarms of patrons, and Gamecocks, standing outside, hands on hips.
Monday, June 28, 2:35 a.m.

#baylerball
Monday, June 28, 9:35 a.m.

RT @MarkSanford Congratulations to the USC Gamecocks on reaching the College World Series finals—all the best tonight
Monday, June 28, 9:43 a.m.

There it is, folks. I'm with Aaron. RT @aaronfitt Wow—Blake Cooper to start tonight. I don't quite get this one.
Monday, June 28, 10:51 a.m.

Two straight starts on 3 days' rest? NO telling. He's tough, but man...RT @RoopertPupkin is Coopers arm ready for tonight?
Monday, June 28, 11:00 a.m.

Just got off phone with Bayler's dad. He says their flight today was canceled. Scheduled to arrive in Omaha at 11 pm tonight, AFTER the game
Monday, June 28, 11:30 a.m.

Anyone know anyone with a plane? (I'm not kidding.)
Monday, June 28, 11:31 a.m.

If you know of anyone with a plane, or know how to make magic happen, let me know. Let's find way to get em here tonight for first pitch!
Monday, June 28, 2:09 p.m.

OK. Teal update: We were able to find charter that can get family to Omaha in time for game. Now we need to come up with $10K to pay for it.
Monday, June 28, 3:46 p.m.

@ashleygilfillan deserves the credit for locating a plane and fronting the bill. Let's show him we appreciate his compassion.
Monday, June 28, 3:50 p.m.

Teal family is on the charter, en route to Omaha!
Monday, June 28, 4:35 p.m.

South Carolina begins its effort for the first meaningful national championship in school history. Right now.
Monday, June 28, 7:38 p.m.

Brady Thomas check-swings a ball down LF line! Huh? Bradley trots in. 1–0 SC. What luck. #baylerball
Monday, June 28, 7:51 p.m.

This brought a huge smile to my face. Guess they're here...RT @ bigeyedfish712 teal family on espn
Monday, June 28, 8:33 p.m.

RT @hollybounds @ashleygilfillan Want to say thanks for what you did to make Teals trip easier. You've given a gift to us all #winforbayler
Monday, June 28, 8:59 p.m.

RT @katemardis UCLA doesnt know theyre playing against an entire state + a new resident of heaven. They dont have a chance #winforbayler
Monday, June 28, 9:05 p.m.

The fact that Cooper carried a no-hitter into the 5th is freaking stunning. Third start in 8 days. #winforbayler
Monday, June 28, 9:42 p.m.

I will bow to Blake Cooper after the game. And tell him I'm sorry for doubting him/Tanner. 7 K's now here in 6th.
Monday, June 28, 9:59 p.m.

Cooper strikes out his 10th to end perfect eighth. I've never seen anything like this. I say that every night here, seems like. #inawe
Monday, June 28, 10:42 p.m.

There it is. Fly ball to Merrifield is final out. FINAL: South Carolina 7, UCLA 1. Gamecocks up 1-0 in this best-of-three.
Monday, June 28, 11:11 p.m.

Gamecocks just won for Bayler. He's still with 'em. One more means a title. #winforbayler
Monday, June 28, 11:19 p.m.

This will come as little surprise to those that know him: Ray Tanner tells me he'll contribute greatly to Teal travel fund. What a man.
Tuesday, June 29, 12:12 a.m.

Grounder to Haney finishes off inning. Roth has given up a run in 5 innings. SC woulda signed on for that in HEARTBEAT. 1–0 UCLA. Halfway.
Thursday, June 29, 9:15 p.m.

He's not going to throw a CG tonight, but give Roth a LOT of credit. Think about it, people: He's given up 2 runs in 14 inn in 2 starts!
Tuesday, June 29, 9:16 p.m.

This is weird game: Lot of nervous SC energy, uncommon to SC team. Yet a 1–0 game. Still time, but 6 outs remaining. Bruins pen tough.
Tuesday, June 29, 10:17 p.m.

Haney grounds it to right side, and UCLA shaky D shows up again. E4 scores Beary from second and we're tied.
Tuesday, June 29, 10:31 p.m.

We are tied. 1–1. There's a new energy in the building. And it's not the wave.
Tuesday, June 29, 10:32 p.m.

South Carolina again has a chance to close Rosenblatt with a walkoff. And with a #winforbayler.
Tuesday, June 29, 11:20 p.m.

For the 10th, Gamecocks have their hats on straight again. Sullivan back in control of the Avatar Spirit Stick. On top step. Clutching it.
Tuesday, June 29, 11:23 p.m.

Anyone know a good ulcer specialist in Columbia?
Tuesday, June 29, 11:37 p.m.

Wingo-Marzilli-Merrifield coming to plate in 11th for Gamecocks. A run wins it. Again. How many chances you want, SC?
Tuesday, June 29, 11:45 p.m.

Wingo works a leadoff walk in 11th. Well done there. Top of lineup coming up. Marzilli will TRY to bunt Wingo to second.
Tuesday, June 29, 11:49 p.m.

Passed ball gets Wingo to second. Didn't need the bunt. Gamecocks are two bases from a national title. 0 out.
Tuesday, June 29, 11:50 p.m.

Marzilli darn-near beats out the bunt. Wingo scoots down to third. Gamecocks have title-winning run on third base, 1 down.
Tuesday, June 29, 11:53 p.m.

Merrifield up now. Fly ball wins a national championship, Whit.
Tuesday, June 29, 11:53 p.m.

Sullivan, on a knee, has the Avatar Spirit Stick.
Tuesday, June 29, 11:54 p.m.

Merrifield ahead in count 2-0. Klein is gassed.
Tuesday, June 29, 11:55 p.m.

That's it. THAT IS IT.
Tuesday, June 29, 11:55 p.m.

South Carolina. You have your national title. It's yours.
Tuesday, June 29, 11:56 p.m.

Whit Merrifield slaps 2-0 pitch into right field. Scott Wingo, who walked, jogs in with the winning run.
Tuesday, June 29, 11:56 p.m.

Rob, Risha and Bridges Teal were here to watch South Carolina win a national championship for their son. Damn, there are those tears again.
Tuesday, June 29, 11:58 p.m.

My gosh. South Carolina just won a national championship.
Wednesday, June 30, 12:47 a.m.

Whit Merrifield's first words to Rob Teal after the game: "I felt Bayler's hand on my bat."
Wednesday, June 30, 1:00 a.m.

ABOUT THE AUTHOR

Travis Haney has covered University of South Carolina sports for *The (Charleston, South Carolina) Post and Courier* since April 2007. Prior to that, he traveled with the Atlanta Braves, covering more than four hundred Major League games for Morris News Service in two-plus seasons.

Haney, twenty-nine, has won numerous writing awards and had a 2004 feature story published in the *Best American Sports Writing* series. The 2003 graduate of the University of Tennessee lives in Columbia, South Carolina, and considers the 2010 College World Series the greatest event he has ever covered, thanks in large part to the Gamecocks' dramatic run to the national title.

The Gamecocks show off the NCAA trophy just after winning the College World Series by sweeping UCLA in the championship series. It was the first national title for a men's program in South Carolina's one-hundred-plus-year athletic history.

Visit us at
www.historypress.net

CPSIA information can be obtained
at www.ICGtesting.com
Printed in the USA
LVHW081250250620
658978LV00001B/1